Contents

A sense of WORDS

knowledge about language in the primary school

John Haynes

Hodder & Stoughton
LONDON SYDNEY AUCKLAND

For Graham Quinn, Sue Johnson, Ian Grosvenor, Susheela Curtiss and friends and colleagues at Sandwell, 1988–90

And for Ainsworth Wright, aged 10, who came from that 'Third World' at the same time as me – with thanks for his many many tales about Anansi.

ACKNOWLEDGMENTS

The publishers would like to thank the following organisations for permission to reproduce copyright material:

HMSO, *passim*; *The Sun* for the extract on p. 13; Routledge and Kegan Paul for the extract on p. 29; BBC Magazines for the extract on p. 37; Longman for the extract on p. 69.

British Library Cataloguing in Publication Data
Haynes, John
    A sense of words: knowledge about language in the
    primary school.
    I. Title
    372.601

    ISBN 0–340 54244–6

First published 1992

© 1991 J. Haynes

Typeset by Wearset, Boldon, Tyne and Wear.
Printed in Great Britain for the educational publishing division of Hodder & Stoughton Ltd, Mill Road, Dunton Green, Sevenoaks, Kent by St Edmundsbury Press Ltd.

Introduction

This book is oriented towards classroom practice. Much of it is devoted to suggesting ways in which children can be encouraged to play with and manipulate language, and in so doing, to begin to formulate ideas for themselves about what language is and how it works. Some of these ideas are set at the level of the reader so that he or she can work through activities analogous to those designed for children.

A fundamental assumption here is that primary teaching and learning is about developing the capacity for exploratory thought, not acquisition of information. If the primary school teacher is a specialist, it is in this. A corollary is that such a teacher's sense of language should be developed dialectically as part of the process of interaction with pupils. Hence, this is not a textbook on applied or diluted linguistics. Rather it is intended to give as much scope as possible for readers to make what they like of it, and to treat it as a starting point for their own thinking and teaching.

The continuous text is accompanied by two types of 'boxes', one plain and one tinted, which suggest a range of classroom-oriented, or teacher-oriented, tasks and activities. The boxes cover the same ground as the continuous text, but in a more open-ended way.

The plain boxes are oriented towards the teacher's own development, and present mainly classroom activities of the type the teacher might give to pupils, but which are pitched at the level of the reader. By working through a typical primary knowledge about language (KAL) problem at their own level, teachers will gain practice in the sort of decisions and problems children have to contend with, and also build up their self-confidence when they find that even without specialised knowledge or jargon they can in fact discover a great deal about how language works, and hopefully find that it is also absorbing.

The tinted boxes are oriented towards children, and contain germs of classroom work to be developed and adapted to a particular class or theme. Both boxes are aimed at sustaining confidence and have practical classroom application. All, in fact, are derived from classroom work which has actually been done. At the same time they open up ways in which ideas about language can develop at the learner's own rate, and according to his or her own way of looking at things, and without the burden of jargon and technicality.

The boxes can serve as exercises or assignments through which the ideas in the continuous text can be explored and evaluated, so long as it is remembered that there are no right or wrong responses to the problems posed in them, beyond those which readers are able to produce to their own satisfaction. The boxes are discontinuous but not random. They form a coherence based on their repetition with variations of both underlying ideas and particular classroom activities, but no attempt has been made to draw attention to this unity. That is left, in the name of collaboration, for readers to think through for themselves.

A second kind of collaboration is implied in the idea that teachers' own knowledge about language can be developed in the process of thinking about and with the children. Indeed, the overall aim of the book is to provide teachers and students with the means, and above all, the attitude which will allow them to both guide and work alongside children in exploring language.

1.1 Making implicit knowledge explicit

1 'I don't know anything about language.'

Yes you do. Look at the following nonsense sentence, and substitute real words for the nonsense ones.

'Grobilly, he's slockling a drep nim about the bodles.'

2 You in fact use a good deal of implicit knowledge about language in making your own sense of this. Consider, and try to make explicit in your own words, in any way you like:

    a How you know that 'slockling' can't mean 'restaurant', 'fire engine', 'red', or 'of course'.

    b How you know which of the following rearrangements are still grammatical, are typical only of poetry or nursery rhymes, or are ungrammatical:

        i Grobilly, I slockle a drep nim about the bodle.
        ii About the bodles, grobilly, he's slockling a drep nim.
        iii Grobilly, he's slockle a drep nims about the bodles.
        iv A nim he's slockling.
        v A nim about the bodle slockles he.
        vi He's bodles the about grobilly drep a nim.

PART ONE

Curriculum, imagination and prejudice

1 | *Approaching knowledge about language*

The scope of knowledge about language

In the widest sense of the term, 'knowledge about language' (or KAL) embraces every aspect of primary school language teaching. Everything a teacher does in this context depends on his or her knowledge about language, from the planning of the language curriculum and the way in which reading and writing are to be taught, to the setting and assessment of individual tasks and activities in class.

This book, however, focuses on the knowledge that children themselves can develop about language, and on the tasks through which they may do so.[1] It is also written for the non-specialist. A fundamental assumption in everything that follows is that teachers without specialist knowledge can evolve their own knowledge about language in the same way, and through the same kinds of tasks, that the children do. This means, put simply, beginning with children's (and teachers') intuitions about language and working towards a more self-conscious awareness and use of them.

What is knowledge about language?

The idea that education should involve a knowledge of how language works is almost as old as western education itself. And courses in language awareness, grammar, communication and language, and so on, have been run long before KAL was introduced in the Kingman and Cox Reports.[2] For what are now practical reasons, reference is made throughout this book to these reports and the ideas related in some detail to *English in the National Curriculum* (ENC), though certainly we need to see KAL in a wider context than that of the recent legislation.[3]

Although KAL includes knowledge about grammar, it includes a good deal more than that, and very little of the work we shall look at will be focused on grammar as such, still less the kind of grammar which used to be taught as linguistic rules and regulations to be followed in writing a formal essay. All too often this kind of work was dispiriting because it concentrated on mistakes, and dull because it was removed from children's experience. It discouraged imagination and flair, and indeed often embodied completely arbitrary prescriptions about English grammar, such as the 'rule' that sentences should not end in prepositions such as 'for' or 'of', or that they should not begin with 'And' or 'But'.

1.2 Traditional grammar

What, in fact, *is* 'a complete sentence'? Attempt a definition, but bear in mind:

a Saying that it is a 'complete thought' is not informative unless you can say what counts as a complete thought.

b Saying that it is whatever comes between full stops is not helpful unless you can explain:

    i how full stops are to be allocated;

    ii what to do about spoken language where there are no full stops.

c Saying it must contain a verb, or even a 'finite' verb, needs to take account of the fact that utterances can have (finite) verbs but still be incomplete.

d Most of the following, surely, are 'complete', so would you call them sentences?

    i Hamlet, Prince of Denmark

    ii EXIT

    iii And in the north-west, here, getting warmer towards midnight.

    iv This Side Up

    v Idiot!

KAL, however, is intended to give children an awareness of language as a means of communication in the very broadest sense, an awareness of how human beings are affected by their use of language, of how a community could not exist without a language, how all our ideas of identity, value and knowledge depend on language, and how languages interact and affect each other. And it aims to bring home to children the ways in which language fits into all our interactions and endeavours, and how it not only enables them to happen but also adapts itself to an almost endless variety of different kinds of interaction, circumstance and media of communication. KAL develops an awareness that children already possess in abundance themselves, as we can see from their rhyming games, their awful puns, tongue-twisters and riddles. KAL aims to show that language is fascinating, fun, and in a far from trivial sense that knowledge about language is knowledge about ourselves.

None of us would know anything, and none of us would be a human being if our mothers and fathers had not been able to communicate to us, and had we not learnt how to play a part in an ordinary conversation. But nor would we be able to function in a modern society if we could not read street signs, use the 'blind' language of the telephone, read the gas bill, the recipe, the album sleeve, and so on. And each of these kinds of communication, some spoken, some written, some a mixture of speech, writing and pictures, is adapted to its social environment just as an animal is adapted to its own particular landscape.

In a sense, the grammatical structure of a language is its core, but we shall not understand this by fixing our minds narrowly on it and it alone, certainly not as a rule book of 'thou-shalt-nots'. The grammatical core of a language is as it is because it has to do all these different things. The most striking fact about a language is that its grammar can simultaneously convey information about the world, express a speaker's attitude or evaluation or emotion, and form these into a coherent stream of utterance appropriate to time, place and circumstance. And language does all these things because we, ordinary people, want and need it to. If we want to change it, we can, and throughout history we have.

1.3 Text and context

1 The immediate environment of a piece of language for actual use (a 'text') is its 'context'. Look at the following piece of an imagined text and underline the parts which only make full sense if you know the context.

> *'No, he didn't. It was over there, look, by your own.'*

2 Work with two or three partners. Each person individually rewrites the quotation with the minimal alterations to make it comprehensible to someone without prior knowledge of the context.

3 Compare your versions, concentrating on:
  a points of similarity;
  b differences.

4 Describe in your own terms (do *not* use any technical terms you may know) the kinds of words you had to introduce to make things clear.

5 What does this exercise suggest to you about the way language is hooked into the physical world?

KAL in the National Curriculum

KAL is not a separate attainment target (AT). It forms a dimension of all. 'Opportunies for the development of children's knowledge about language exist *in all key stages* and all ATs.'[4]

Some strands in *English in the National Curriculum* refer specifically to KAL. These strands are the ones added in the second Cox Report on Kenneth Baker's request. They begin at level 5, at the end of Key Stage 2, but this does not mean that KAL is to be taught only at the top of the junior school without groundwork having been laid earlier. The development of literacy involves a good deal of explicit teaching about language. Learning to spell and read, for example, involve learning explicitly what letters and words are, and that they are connected to speech sounds and to meanings.[5]

KAL and continuity

KAL must be looked at on a whole-school basis because it implies attitudes to language which need to be developed from the beginning of schooling, and to be demonstrated in practice long before children are asked to reflect upon it. They can, after all, hardly be expected to believe that 'ain't' is not 'bad English' when throughout their infant school years they have been told it is, and made to feel embarrassed for saying it.[6]

KAL and the functional view of language

Kingman, Cox and ENC all advocate the study of language through meaning and context. They recommend this study to begin with what language does in a real life context, what the purposes of the speakers or writers are, how they are affected by the setting, and whether the language is written or spoken. Rather than beginning with small details out of context, first let us look at the context, and then see how the details function within that context, what their point and purpose is (see the statements of attainment shown opposite).

This functional view of language has been explored most fully by the linguist M. A. K. Halliday whose work we will draw upon in a number of ways, but in particular in the emphasis that will be placed on thinking in terms of (spoken and written) texts.[7] Indeed, one way of summing up KAL, and distinguishing it from older more scholastic approaches to the study of language, would be to say that it is primarily the study of texts, and that texts are the means through which human beings relate to each other.

Explicit and implicit knowledge about language

The Kingman Report distinguishes between implicit and explicit KAL. KAL is explicit when the children can describe aspects of a text such as how, as a spoken text, it differs from a similar written text. It is implicit when the children are intuitively aware of how the text is constructed, and can follow text-making rules, though they may not be able fully to articulate what those rules are. And Kingman recommends that the independent assessment of work in KAL be based on intuitive or practical KAL, not on the explicit statement of rules.

Cox is less detailed in this particular area, and the wording of Cox is modified in ENC, so that the distinction between explicit (articulated) and implicit (practical) KAL is blurred. In Cox, children are required, for example to 'talk about variations in vocabulary between different regional or social groups'[8]; but in ENC 'talk about' has become 'recognise'.[9]

The ambiguous 'recognise' marks out an indeterminate stage between 'knowing how' and 'knowing that'. This poses a central problem for the assessment of KAL because it leaves undefined the degree of explicitness required.

But from the point of view of teaching, the ambiguity marks out the area in which children's KAL develops. Learning about language can only develop as a process from knowing how, towards, and as a basis for, knowing that; from practical problem solving in language in which the children formulate their own terminology as and when needed, towards the use of standard terms such as 'sentence', 'cohesion', 'tense' and so on. In the primary school the emphasis falls on laying the foundation in problem solving and developing an exploratory questioning attitude to language.

6.22 In the **SPEAKING AND LISTENING PROFILE COMPONENT** pupils should be able to:

LEVEL	DESCRIPTION
5	Talk about variations in vocabulary between different regional or social groups, *eg dialect vocabulary, specialist terms.*
6	Talk about some grammatical differences between spoken Standard English and a non-standard variety.
7	Talk about appropriateness in the use of spoken language, according to purpose, topic and audience, *eg differences between language appropriate to a job interview and to a discussion with peers.*
8	Talk about the contribution that facial expressions, gestures and tone of voice can make to a speaker's meaning, *eg in ironic and sarcastic uses of language.*
9	Talk about ways in which language varies between different types of spoken communication, *eg joke, anecdote, conversation, commentary, lecture.*
10	Talk about some of the factors that influence people's attitudes to the way other people speak.

6.23 In the **WRITING PROFILE COMPONENT** pupils should be able to:

LEVEL	DESCRIPTION
5	Talk about variations in vocabulary according to purpose, topic and audience and according to whether language is spoken or written, *eg slang, formal vocabulary, technical vocabulary.*
6	Demonstrate some knowledge of straightforward grammatical differences between spoken and written English.
7	Comment on examples of appropriate and inappropriate use of language in written texts, with respect to purpose, topic and audience.
8	Demonstrate some knowledge of organisational differences between spoken and written English.
9	Demonstrate some knowledge of ways in which language varies between different types of written text, *eg peronal letter, formal letter, printed instructions, newspaper report, playscript.*
10	Demonstrate some knowledge of criteria by which different types of written language can be judged, *eg clarity, coherence, accuracy, appropriateness, effectiveness, vigour etc.*

6.24 In the **READING PROFILE COMPONENT** pupils should be able to:

LEVEL	DESCRIPTION
5	Recognise and talk about the use of word play, *eg puns, unconventional spellings etc,* and some of the effects of the writer's choice of words in imaginative uses of English.
6	Talk about examples (from their own experience or from their reading) of changes in word use and meaning over time, and about some of the reasons for these changes, *eg technological developments, euphemism, contact with other languages, fashion.*
7	Talk about some of the effects of sound patterning, *eg rhyme, alliteration,* and figures of speech, *eg similes, metaphors, personification,* in imaginative uses of English.
8	Identify in their reading, and talk and write about some of the changes in the grammar of English over time, *eg in pronouns (from thou and thee to you), in verb forms, in negatives, etc.*
9	Demonstrate some understanding of the use of special lexical and grammatical effects in literary language, *eg the repetition of words or structures, dialect forms, archaisms, grammatical deviance etc.*
10	Demonstrate some understanding of attitudes in society towards language change and of ideas about appropriateness and correctness in language use.

1.4 Devising terminology

1 KAL is *not* about technical terms. Look at the following:
  a Sherjit visited Amanda
  b Sherjit and Amanda went out
  c Sherjit was visited by Amanda
  d Sherjit went to visit Amanda but didn't find her and came back
  e Sherjit didn't visit Amanda

2 Rewrite each of these without using words except for the names of the people. Everying else must be symbolised by arrows, which can be varied in any way you like.

3 Exchange versions with a partner and translate each other's arrow grammar back into the original forms.

4 How many kinds of arrow have you had to use? Can they be reduced to a smaller number? Devise descriptive names for each kind.

Notes

1 In this, the focus differs from that of the LINC materials developed primarily for the education of teachers, and oriented towards knowledge a teacher needs to plan programmes.

2 *Report of the Committee of Inquiry into the Teaching of English Language* (DES, 1988) (Kingman Report). London: HMSO.

  The Kingman Report derived from the Bullock Report – *A Language for Life* (DES, 1975), Report of the Committee of Inquiry appointed by the Secretary of State for Education and Science. London: HMSO.

  The Kingman Report informs the Cox Report, which lays the foundation for *English in the National Curriculum*. Reference will be made to the second Cox Report, in which KAL receives special attention at the request of the Secretary of State. This is *English for ages 5 to 16* (1989). Proposals of the Secretary of State for Education and Science and the Secretary of State for Wales. London: HMSO.

3 And indeed to see the limitations of Kingman, Cox and ENC. The authors of *Patterns of Learning* point out that ENC is a statement of a minimum curriculum, which leaves out a great deal that good English teachers would normally include, and which lacks an overall unity, which again, teachers need to provide. See *Patterns of Learning* by Myra Barrs, Sue Ellis, Hilary Hester, and Anne Thomas (London: Centre for Language in Primary Education, 1990). This book is a follow-up to the widely used *The Primary Language Record* published by the same authors and publisher (then CLPE/ILEA), which has been very influential, and a number of whose ideas on planning, assessing and record keeping were adopted by the Cox Committee, and incorporated in ENC.

4 *English Non-Statutory Guidance* (1990). National Curriculum Council, p. D7.

5 A difference between the Cox and Kingman Reports is that in Kingman greater attention is given to the need for KAL in the development of literacy.

6 The appropriateness of KAL in Key Stage 1 is illustrated in *Patterns of Learning*. The interlacing paths of development include one called 'knowledge and understanding', in which a number of strands in levels 1, 2 and 3 are entered. See the diagram in *Patterns of Language* on p. 27.

7 The most readable of Halliday's books, and the most relevant to KAL is *Language as Social Semiotic*. This book is made up of a number of essays. The first, an interview in which Halliday explains his approach, makes a good and accessible starting point for the reader without prior knowledge of linguistics. A series of books for teachers, based on Halliday's approach, is edited by

Frances Christie, who is the author of the excellent and unjargoned introductory volume, *Language Education* (Oxford University Press, 1989). In the same series is Halliday's *Spoken and Written Language* (London: Oxford University Press, 1985), and slightly more demanding but very important for KAL, is *Language, Context and Text* by M A K Halliday and R Hasan (London: Oxford University, 1989). The reader might also find *Introducing Stylistics* by John Haynes (London: Unwin Hyman, 1989) worth dipping into.

8 *English for ages 5 to 16* (DES, 1989), para. 6.22. London: HMSO.
9 Attainment Target 1, level 5(e) in *English in the National Curriculum* DES, p. 4 (London: HMSO).

2 | *On not being all that good at grammar*

An exploratory approach to KAL

As a child, or as an adult, as a pupil or as a teacher it is possible at any level to plunge into the exploration of language and enjoy it. Most people are in fact fascinated by language. Think of children's unforced interest in riddles, tongue-twisters, jokes and of the role of word play in children's games, and songs, their fascination with secret codes, and so on.

2.1 Text collage

1 Task

Children work in groups. The teacher takes turns to join each group and work with them. They must make up a message to send to another group. The message must:

    a   relate to a topic they are already working on; or

    b   use only

        i   non-verbal symbols from The Highway Code (or another similar source);

        ii words that they can see displayed on the classroom walls.

2 Assessment

    a   What did you, as the teacher, learn about texts and messages from working on the task with the children?

    b   List the main unorthodox interpretations of The Highway Code, and classroom notices, that you had to use.

    c   How are the messages devised in class like and/or unlike those in an ordinary language?

2.2 Children's knowledge about language

1 Joke riddles

Question: Where does a frog hang up its coat?

Answer: In a croak room!

2   What do the children have (implicitly) to recognise about words, word associations, and contexts, to understand this riddle?

3   Devise five different classroom tasks making use of joke riddles and the implicit KAL they use. Consider the use of rhyme, and the close similarity between 'cr' and 'cl', and how other similarities of this kind might be used, e.g. 'st/str', 'b/br/bl'.

The most important single goal a teacher can bear in mind is to help children to find language fun, and ultimately a source of wonder. To achieve this teachers need to take an open-minded attitude towards it, and not let themselves be inhibited by solemnity. It is necessary to stress this because until recently, under the heading of 'grammar', children have been subjected to a very dry analysis of sentences taught in the name of 'training the mind' but in fact embodying large amounts of narrow prejudice and coercion.

The reaction to this in Britain, shortly after the Second World War, was to withdraw from teaching language structures altogether, which left a generation or two with happier English lessons, but little idea how their mother tongue worked and was developing. Now, when, partly for political reasons, there is a movement

---

2.3 Prejudice about language
Passage from *The Sun*

It ain't right

A NEW report on grammar, backed by Education Secretary Kenneth Baker, picks out some real howlers:

We was; he ain't done it; she come here yesterday; they never saw nobody.

According to the report, while pupils must write proper English it does not matter if they talk like that.

We could not agree less. It is absurd not to correct children who use bad English. It is a habit that could prevent them getting good jobs.

It does not matter what your accent is – Cockney, Yorkshire, Lancashire or Scottish – as long as WHAT you say is proper English.

The Sun editorial

---

1   What does the writer mean by 'bad English' and 'proper English'?

2   What is the origin of the term 'howler'? What overall view of language learning does it suggest?

3   What view of speakers who say 'ain't' etc. is implied by the writer's use of the word 'habit'?

4   What is wrong with saying 'we was'?

6   How far does the passage correspond to what is said in the second Cox Report about KAL?

back to explicit teaching about language, many teachers understandably fear that they are going to be asked to put the clock back to laying down the law about not beginning sentences with some words and not ending them with others, dangling particles, split infinitives, and the rest.[1]

However, the old prejudices about 'good English' and so on persist, and are rehearsed almost daily in the media.[2] They persist, in part, because there has been no worked-out approach to KAL after the abandonment of old-style grammar. Teachers who do want to get children to look at and into language find they have no tools and so fall back on the earlier practices. For this reason it is necessary to say a little more about them.

2.4 Incomplete sentences

ENC echoes traditional grammar in referring to 'complete sentences'. But how do we recognise these? How do children?

The following are incomplete in the sense that they depend on the reader already knowing something about the context. For each example make a brief statement of what this contextual knowledge or prior experience is:

a   That's not the one.
b   A stitch in time saves nine.
c   Dogs must be carried.
d   f.y.i.a.
e   Once upon a time there lived a huge wicked giant.

How might you use examples like this to develop children's:

a   Knowledge about genre?
b   Reading strategies other than phonics?
c   Ideas for structuring a story?

'Good' English

The idea that there are different qualities of English is based on the prejudice that there is something special about the 'Queen's English', or 'BBC English', or 'Educated English'. What has happened, historically, is that a section of speakers of English has managed to convince others that their dialect is especially valuable, and should be taken as the standard by which all others are judged. Consequently any use of English which differs from the standard dialect becomes down-graded as 'bad' or 'incorrect'.

The high status which educated south-eastern English has attained is connected to the concentration of power in London, and among an educated class of people who bring up their children to speak this dialect, wherever they come from. The status of standard English as 'good' English is thus primarily a political and social matter. The most powerful people in the country have generally controlled the education system, and hence the kind of English favoured in that system has been the kind of English they speak themselves and so see as preferable.

In addition to this there was the model of Latin. In the past all educated people were educated in Latin, and a great deal of time was given to acquiring a command of correct – that is written – Latin, which had to be learned consciously and with explicit teaching of grammar. As the English language became more prominent in public and educated life, it was felt that the method of looking at Latin grammar should be applied to English, which came to be taught as if it were a foreign, and 'dead' language. Grammarians searched for Latin-like rules to apply to English, and in the process tried to impose a kind of grammar on English which was really only appropriate to Latin.

In reality, from the point of view of the study of language as such, rather than from the point of view of language politics, *there is no such thing as 'good' English*, at least not in the sense that one person's dialect or use of grammar is intrinsically better than anyone else's. Saying 'ain't' is not 'bad English'. Nor are there fixed rules; there are simply descriptions of the way people of all kinds actually speak under all kinds of circumstances. The goodness or badness of English can only be assessed on the basis of how well a particular speaker or writer actually communicates under particular circumstances.

This is the approach to English taken in the Kingman Report, and in the two Cox Reports, and which informs *English in the National Curriculum* (ENC). The KAL component of ENC entails a rejection of traditional grammar teaching and gives scope for enjoying language and developing a sense of fun and wonder about it.[3] Earlier generations of language teachers approached their work in an authoritarian way which led them to stress a range of 'rules to be obeyed', and getting the rules wrong was not just making a mistake; unorthodox ways of speaking were seen as 'ignorant' and 'vulgar', and getting them wrong was a source of embarrassment and shame. Children who spoke with a Cockney or Geordie accent, or used rural dialect words, were made to feel inferior, and the normal speech of their family and friends was insulted and disparaged. This made the classroom an alien place in which children's dignity was trampled on. Better not to open your mouth.

In approaching the development of KAL in the primary school the first thing teachers must do is to rid themselves of prejudices about correct and proper English. For the moment, priority will be given simply to taking our own and children's language just as it is, as a fascinating fact of life.

Language and 'logic'

After all if expressions like 'I ain't doin nuffin' really were illogical or unintelligible they would have died out long ago because the people who used them would have confused *each other* as to what they meant. If some accents really were 'ugly' or 'incomprehensible', then surely the speakers themselves would have noticed something amiss! People have spent whole lives using them and might have noticed if in all that time they had never been understood.

2.5 Double negatives

1 Context

A parent returns home to find that the jellies and cakes for a party have been either eaten or trodden on.

2 Text

Parent What've you done?
Child I never done nothing!
Parent You never done nothing?
Child The dog done it.
Parent You let the dog in?
Child He came in.
Parent And where was you?
Child I was watching telly, wasn't I?
Parent You was watching telly!
Child Yeah.
Parent And right next to you the dog was on the table?
Child Never noticed it.
Parent Eating jellies, and trifles, and . . . You just sat there.
Child (*Shrugs*)
Parent And never done nothing.
Child That's what I told you. I never done nothing.

3 Work with a partner and try to formulate for yourself:

a The two different senses in which 'I never done nothing' is used.

b How they are distinguished when you act them on tape.

c How the use of 'never' could not in fact be confused with SE (Standard English) usage.

d What difference it would make if this text used 'anything' instead of 'nothing'.

It used to be said that double negatives were 'illogical'. But illogical on what basis? Is English *spelling* illogical? When a child, very logically writes 'yot' for 'yacht' they seem to have logic on their side, but now they are wrong. It seems as if the goalposts have been moved. In fact what we count as 'logical' depends on the criteria we use. 'Yot' is logical compared with 'got' and 'lot', but if the origins of the word, in Dutch, are born in mind, then it is 'logical' to spell it in such a way as to show its source. In fact, appeals to 'logic' in general terms can seldom be taken too seriously in studying language.

Language has its own patterns and these are no more or no less logical than other aspects of our experience, like flowers, or fashion, or love. Rather than looking for 'logic' in the abstract we should be looking for patterns and then for a 'logic' to each pattern.

2.6 Logic and language

Discuss the following examples with a partner. Which forms are logical and which are illogical?

1 a I burnt myself   (SE)
   b He burnt hisself   (Hereford)
   c I burnt meself   (Devon)
2 a You like it, don't you?   (SE)
   b Tu l'aimes, n'est ce pas?   (French)
   c You like it, isn't it?   (Nigeria)

3 a are
   b care
   c car

4 a It's coming.
   b It's raining.

An exploratory approach

This book is composed in the hope that, as it progresses, after trying out its suggestions, and adapting (or scrapping) them, readers can work out their own approach to KAL, developing their ideas in just the way the children will, based on their own terms, interests and sense of what is going on – in short, being themselves.

It cannot be denied that a detailed and enthusiastic knowledge of language is a great advantage to a primary teacher. But not everyone can be a specialist. The approach to KAL is parallel to the approach to games by a primary school teacher who is not a specialist in PE. Many teachers, asked to teach a games session using hockey sticks or rugby balls may, quite wrongly, feel inadequate for lack of specialist knowledge. They do not know the rules in any detail. But, then, teaching detailed specific skills would be inappropriate anyway. After all the aim is to educate the children about games as such, team cooperation, self-control, and so on, not to train them to get into this or that team. What is required in PE here is not *specialist instruction* of how to do a spinning rugby pass, or bully off. What is required is an *understanding* of the basic principles of the game, and even more generally the broad kind of game in which one team has to devise tactics to invade the territory of the other.

This chapter is, therefore, devoted to a combination of reassurance and challenge, or rather a challenge in the form of a reassurance: the teacher does not need to have detailed knowledge of the technical terms of linguistics to teach language awareness in the primary school. This point can hardly be over-emphasised. Nor, of course, can it be over-emphasised that it is wholly inappropriate for children in a primary school to learn formal grammatical analysis for its own sake, or technical jargon that is not their own technical jargon. Technical terms are only useful when the pupil has rummaged about in language sufficiently enjoyably to need and *want* some shorthand or to make some

2.7 Grammar without terminology

Level and context

This particular work is set at top junior level, and would need adapting to fit with the particular topic the children are doing, so that the example would have a context.

1 Photocopy and cut out the following word groups in the shapes shown or, instead of shapes, substitute different coloured cards (as shown in brackets).

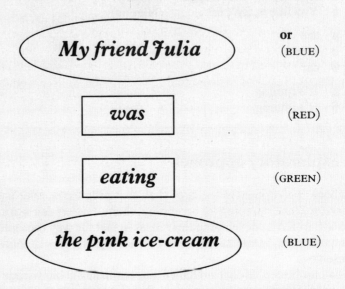

My friend Julia   **or** (BLUE)

was   (RED)

eating   (GREEN)

the pink ice-cream   (BLUE)

2 Arrange the strips to make different utterances. Any combination is acceptable so long as you can think of a context in which it would make sense. Do as many as you can:
   a using all the groups;
   b leaving out one or more;
   c using all the word groups in such a way that they can be followed by an extra (oval or blue) group, 'happy' as the last item in the utterance.

3 Record your versions and arrange them according to whether they are:
   a informing somebody about something;
   b asking a question;
   c giving a command;
   d exclaiming;
   e making an offer;
   f those which would only occur in spoken language, or written imitations of speech.

4 Turn the cards over so that the wording cannot be seen. Invent other utterances substituting your own wording for the particular shaped (coloured) cards.

generalisations, and to save the trouble of writing out long descriptions. Indeed, creating technical terms and abbreviations is itself a productive KAL activity for children. But in the primary school it is much more valuable to use home-made terms, just as in maths where children begin with non-standard kinds of measures, so that by working through the problems of describing in their own language, they really make their understanding their own.

Rather than teaching spinning passes and other detailed techniques – the 'grammar of rugby', the 'grammar of hockey' – what is required is putting the children into a position where they themselves have to devise the rules for an invasion game. What are the conditions which allow them to have an enjoyable game without people running into the changing hut with the ball, or threatening to hit others with the hockey stick?[4] What possibilities does this peculiar shaped ball or this queer hooked stick open up? In language work, the same sorts of questions are asked. What sorts of wording or gestures or signs will allow us to tell someone who is not there that we want something? How can we communicate something about tomorrow before tomorrow comes? What equivalents to balls or sticks do we have to hand to use for communication?

Instead of homing in on small details, or memorising the names of classes of words, the children must first be put into problematic situations where they have to ask questions and think of answers for themselves, about how language works to communicate. This applies to any learner, not just to children. And the primary goal of this book is to put readers in similar problematic situations, at their own level and on their own terms.[5]

Form, function and process

In making intuitive KAL conscious, we begin, not as in traditional grammar with small pieces of language, but with whole texts and whole contexts. We ask ourselves questions about the ways in which how we speak or write follows from what we are doing in and through speaking or writing. What are our purposes? What are the social conventions we must observe, or flout? What are we addressing, and what impression do we want to make? And so on. These wider purposes a text has are often referred to as its 'functions', whereas the detailed linguistic means are referred to as the 'form'. Thus:

'I love to ride to school in the snow
I like to ride my bike in a blizzard'

has the functions of expressing pleasure, beginning a rap poem, informing the reader or hearer about an experience, entertaining an audience, and perhaps others. When we ask ourselves how the composer expresses these things, then we point to individual aspects of the language. He expresses his enthusiasm by using the word 'love'. He fulfils the poetic function by having four stressed words, and fitting them to a beat, and by near repetition: 'love'/'like', 'snow'/'blizzard'. In the second line the wording functions to make the scene more specific ('blizzard' for 'snow'), and also creates humour by a kind of boastfulness.

Another way of looking at linguistic function is to take a reader's role, and by looking just at the first line, and then being told that the next line 'repeats in different words', to try to guess what the second line will be. The chances are that the prediction will give an alternative fulfilment of the same function.

Most of the work we describe in KAL involves this relation between what the purposes of a text are, and how they are fulfilled; but it also requires that we pay particular attention to the *process* of composition, or of interpretation, or of rehearsal for performance, and discuss this process as we go along.

Notes

1 The first document in which the case was set out is the Kingman Report (1988), *Report of the Committee of Inquiry into the Teaching of English Language* (London: HMSO).

2 See box 2.3.

3 A useful overview of the issues surrounding the Kingman Report, when it was first published, is given in 'Unproductive busy work' by Richard Chandler in *English in Education*, 22, 3, 1988.

4 For this and other ideas drawn from PE I am grateful to Sue Timms, advisory teacher in movement at Sandwell.

5 Which, of course, implies that they do develop and do become knowledgeable about language. The reassurances to the non-specialist given above should not be taken as an acceptance of *continuing ignorance about language*. Kingman and others have stressed the need for more time to be devoted to KAL in teacher education – see Chapter 17.

3 | *Justifications for knowledge about language*

Kenneth Baker's insistence on KAL could be seen as a gesture towards popular prejudices about grammar and 'good English'. But there are, also, valid educational reasons for its inclusion in the primary school curriculum; though these are not very well articulated in either the Kingman or the Cox Reports.[1]

Justifications for KAL in Cox and Kingman

There are variations in detail, but Cox and Kingman make essentially the same points. These are summed up by Cox as follows:

> 'Two justifications for teaching pupils explicitly about language are, first, the positive effect on aspects of their use of language and secondly, the general value of such knowledge as an important part of their understanding of their social and cultural environment, since language has vital functions in the life of the individual and of society.'[2]

These two justifications may be summed up as the *cultural* and the *enabling* justifications.

The cultural justification for KAL

The Kingman Report refers to the development of ideas in the philosophical and academic study of language which have placed it in a central position. Writers in the fields of semiotics (the general study of symbolic meanings) have developed the new widely held idea that we live in a 'textual' world. Everything that we do is affected by language, and our perceptions of the world and society, and indeed of ourselves, is conditioned by the way in which these are presented to us in language, and other symbolic systems. But when we use one of these symbolic systems to communicate something that seems to us simply factual or common-sense, we seldom are being as neutral as we think. We are seeing things from a particular angle deriving from our background, experience, including what we have been told and read. Even our notion of ourselves is much less within our own decision than we may believe.[3]

Since this is a difficult idea and apt to sound bizarre when stated in general terms, especially from the perspective of the primary school classroom, it may be useful to look at it more closely. Imagine we begin telling *The Ugly Duckling* to a group of middle infant children. We introduce this picture as we read:

Then, after that, or later in the day, we read a Brer Rabbit story. We introduce the following picture:

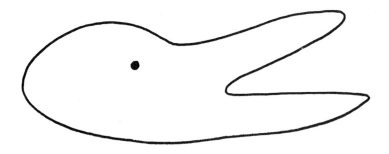

First it is a duck, then a rabbit. The question now arises, 'How can it be that the same picture can have two meanings?' What pushed us into seeing it in one way rather than in another was the way in which the image was presented in language. Language is interpretative and affects our understanding of what we see, what is real, what is 'obvious', what seems like common-sense.

When we work on this theme with children, one of our aims will be to put them in a position to recognise this themselves, that interpreting what is 'before our very eyes' is very much a linguistic matter, and perhaps to link this with the presentation of facts and ideas on the media.[4]

The cultural justification of KAL is basically the justification that, in a sense, cultural and ideological values are carried by language.[5] Television provides a very striking example of this, but it can be drawn out of the study of children's own casual conversations and play; and indeed, in that of teachers too. Stereotypes of gender, race, occupation, and class, are carried by the most everyday language.

An important dimension of this is the way in which language is used to exclude. It is easy to laugh at outsiders. The Jamaican boy who says 'me know' gets jibes from his classmates. But then, in the Black Country, they themselves will say, 'her knows'. Should they themselves, then, be laughed at by the speaker of standard English? Why do we laugh at other people's accents? Why do they laugh at ours? Raising these questions raises the issue of insularity and chauvinism which is

3.1 Caption and angle

1 Photos of 'facts'
The children are given a set of photographs taken from newspapers or magazines dealing with topics they have talked about in class and/or are interested in.

2 Angle
The teacher then gives them captions and speech bubbles to match to the pictures, but none is a straightforward 'factual' description. Whatever caption or bubble they fit will amount to all oblique reference to or comment on the photo. The choice of pictures and comments depends on age and topics being studied.

3 Examples

Picture	*Caption/bubble that might be matched*
Totally rundown street	'Britshire has a low poll tax'
Anguished sportsperson	'Where's the toilet?'

4 Children's work
Children discuss the matchings they have devised in their groups, and work out oral explanations as to what the unstated point of each one is.

5 Development
   a They begin collecting their own media photos and keep an angle and caption book, 'ideological joke book'.

   b They extend the work into other kinds of word play such as inventing riddles by starting with the caption and then finding an angled picture as the 'solution'.

---

particularly closely associated with language in Britain. Then we have to ask why a particular dialect should have become so widely understood that it is used for the national news, and why should it have higher status than the way most people speak at home? This raises the issue of power and prompts questions about the origins of that power. Where did standard English come from? Where did Black Country English come from? Or Jamaican English?[6]

Language is often used not just to promote a particular point of view, or as a status symbol, but to control people. This is particularly clear in schools. Much of the teacher's own language has this function. Terms like 'good', 'naughty', 'lazy', 'able', and 'hardworking' are used to enforce the teacher's power, to control the class, and at the same time to lay down a set of textual roles for the children to play.[7]

An interesting question here is how far children should be made aware of the rhetorical games their teachers plays in order to manipulate them, and what the goals are. The main skill in using language to control others is, as far as possible, to avoid direct threat and present the desired way of behaving as the natural normal common-sense way, and to make the coercion as unobtrusive as possible. Teachers tend to reserve a direct show of power and explicit control for crises, and to depend on building up a routine for activities in which there is a given way of doing things properly. The control exercised by television cannot, of course, be like this, because television sets, unlike teachers, can be switched off. Yet the influence of television on children's attitudes is at least comparable to that of the classroom.

3.2 Language and power

1 Drama

The children work in threes rehearsing a drama in which Mr/Ms Powerful is demanding food or some other service from Mr/Ms Powerless. Powerful hectors, abuses, and above all commands, and is always trying to catch out Powerless. Powerless is obsequious and ultra polite. The third member of the group is the director. The roles are rotated.

2 Language

The actors thus need to bear in mind:
- a body language of dominance and obsequiousness;
- b speech acts (commanding versus appeasing);
- c vocabulary and voice tones.
- d Powerless in particular must be able to guess from his/her body language what Powerful is about to say, and be ready to respond or forestall.

3 Plot

Hint at or give the children the idea that at first Powerless needs Powerful because he is employed by him as a servant, and fears being sacked and made penniless. But then Powerless gradually realises that Powerful needs him more, and could not replace him. Hence the roles become reversed with Powerful begging Powerless to stay, and Powerless dictating terms.

Some teachers may see the whole idea of making children aware of the mechanisms by which they are controlled difficult and potentially subversive of their position. But if part of the school ethos is taken to be linguistic self-awareness, being critical, noticing the biased interpretation, the loaded example, the hidden evaluation, then this way of looking at lingustically carried power can be a productive part of the curriculum, especially as school discourses are such clear-cut examples of language used to control and influence.

Self-consciousness about interaction and ideological slant are no more than touched upon in the Kingman Report, but the names of semioticians cited, particularly Derrida, imply the approach outlined here.[8] The particular interpretation to be placed on the cultural component of KAL will vary with the ideological position of the teacher (and parents) of course. Not all teachers, for example, will be comfortable encouraging the children to question and discuss the values implicit in the running of the classroom. Why do we have to do our maths now? Why can't we do drawing now and maths later? Why do I have to do what all the others are doing? Why do we have to line up? And so on. And some headteachers may not relish having their assembly stories subjected to ideological analysis by the top juniors. They may prefer to limit the negotiable areas. The point to see is that this area of reviewing talk, both from the teachers, and among peers, is very fertile. We need to remember that questioning and scepticism form the basis of the scientific culture within which this discussion is placed, and the sorts of attitudes expected in a democracy.

3.3 Your own language of control

1 Work with a fellow teacher or student and record yourselves taking a class. Make a note of your own utterances which are aimed at:
    a directly controlling the children's behaviour;
    b indirectly controlling the children's behaviour;
    c individuals, groups, or the whole class.

2 With your partner, classify the way you use language to achieve control. Use any set of categories you think useful, but bear in mind how far you may have conned the children.

3 Compare your own strategies with those of your partner, and attempt to formulate the implicit rules your language of control entails. This may not necessarily be the same as your beliefs.

An understanding of the language of control need not necessarily be subversive or destructive. If children feel that they have a genuine say themselves in controlling what happens in the classroom, they are more likely to commit themselves to making it work.

The cultural justification for KAL, then, is that it allows children to see how language is used in a culture, to present a particular viewpoint, to promote solidarity, to exclude 'outsiders', and more fundamentally to see how language is used to control people, themselves included.

The aesthetic justification of KAL

The idea that KAL can improve linguistic performance is controversial. And Cox's invocation of KAL's 'positive effect on aspects of their use of language' remains extremely vague.[9] However, although the question is not seriously addressed in either the Kingman or Cox Reports, in fact, KAL can have an effect on the way children use language, only if KAL is linked to the aesthetic enjoyment of textual patterns and to the communicative force they can have. This implies an approach to language as a source of wonder and interest, and recognising that children already have this in their own way. Indeed the language teacher's problem is not how to *foster* what we shall call an 'aesthetic' approach to language; it is to avoid inadvertently stamping this out.

Thus, rather than referring misleadingly to an 'enabling' justification, the term 'aesthetic' will be used to refer to the relishing of language. Children's interest in language patterning exactly parallels their fascination with patterning to be found in mathematics and in art.

The common-sense traditional approach has been that knowing the theory can help someone get the practice right. The traditional grammar teacher explains that 'their' is different from 'there' and 'they're'; tests the class, and hopes that henceforth they will get it right. Traces of this have been detected in ENC.[10] But as long ago as 1947 research showed that teaching formal grammar had little effect, and the results have since been confirmed.[11]

The original impetus behind the teaching of formal grammar in our culture, in ancient Greece, came from the colonial situation in which non-native speakers of Greek, in Macedonia, for example, needed to be coached so that they could communicate reports in the conquerors' language. That is, it originated as a problem in foreign language teaching. Later, in Britain, this was taken into the education system in which Greek and Latin were the core subjects and their grammar taught explicitly, again as foreign, now 'dead', languages, and in written form.

Later, because people greatly admired Latin and Greek and thought them superior languages to their native English, they began to apply the methods of studying those languages to English itself, and so English became subject to grammatical analysis, but to a kind of analysis which had been devised to suit Greek and Latin. It did not suit English, but was nevertheless forced into service, and English structures understood as if they were poor attempts to match up to Latin or Greek ones.

Nowadays the attempt to fit English into the straitjacket of Latin has been dropped. But the pleas for a prescriptive kind of grammar teaching remain. Why is this, since everyone speaks English naturally from a very early age? The answer is that this justification of grammar teaching is aimed not now at a foreign or 'dead' language but at what we might call a 'foreign' dialect.

Where modern children make mistakes in English is where they are asked to speak *a kind of English that they do not normally speak at home*. The dialect concerned is standard English (SE). When the Cox Report refers to this teaching having a 'positive effect on aspects of their use of language', the 'aspects' certainly include the grammar of standard English. And in practice the enabling justification for KAL is aimed primarily at the enhancement of standard English.[12]

For most children there are differences between home and standard English, and complications arise from this. Standard English tends to be based upon the values of written language, and to be associated with writing. So learning to write and read is also learning standard English writing and reading. But there are other kinds of differences between speaking and writing which affect grammar too, and these get drawn into teachers' perceptions of literacy which is closely associated with standard English, since almost all books are written in standard English.

For example, one difference between spoken and written language is that, for most texts that the children will write, a more formal tone is required than for speaking. Interactional phrases such as 'isn't it?' are not considered appropriate in an essay, and written language must be punctuated according to grammatical rules, and composed in 'complete sentences'.

The Cox Report does not revert to traditional 'colonialist' justifications for the use of standard English. It makes the point that different texts have different conventions as to what sorts of grammar and vocabulary are 'appropriate'. Standard English is appropriate, even necessary, for certain kinds of communication, but not all. What children have to learn, then, is what grammar is appropriate to what texts and occasions. And for those occasions where standard English is appropriate they must have it as a part of their linguistic repertoire.

3.4 Dialect and appropriateness
From *Language Barrier* by Valerie Bloom

Jamaica language sweet yoh know bwoy,
An huh me nebba notice i',
Till tarra day one foreign frien'
Come spen some time wid me.

An den im call me attention to
Some tings im sey soun' queer,
Like de way we always seh 'koo hay'
When we really mean 'look here.' . . .

. . . Me advise im no fe fret imself,
For de Spaniards do it to,
For when dem mean fe sey 'jackass'
Dem always sey 'burro'.

(From *Touch Mi Tell Mi* (1983). London: Bogle-L'Ouverture Publications p. 41).

1 Comment on:
   a What makes standard English inappropriate in this text.
   b The point Bloom makes in the last stanza.

2 Why does the spelling of some words differ from standard spelling? Does standard spelling correspond to a particular accent?

3 Pick out the differences in vocabulary from standard English.

4 How does the treatment of pronouns (me, my, he, him, his, etc.) differ from standard English?

5 What does the word 'fe' mean?

'In general terms, we advocate that there should be explicit teaching about the nature and functions of standard English in the top years of the primary school.' (Cox: 4.38)

And this should be done in connection with both written and spoken English but not in a didactic way so as to make children whose home dialect is not standard English feel that the speech of their families is being criticised.

'The aim is to add standard English to the repertoire, not to replace other dialects or languages.' (Cox: 4.43)

And

'Standard English should form an important part of the teaching of knowledge about language: its historical, geographical and social distribution and the uses to which it is put (in different countries, in different areas of society, in print and in the mass media, etc.). Teachers should encourage an interest in both rural (traditional) and urban dialects of English . . . The grammar of both should be discussed and contrasted. Non-standard usages should be treated as objects of interest and value, and not ridiculed.' (Cox: 4.42)[13]

An example of the aesthetic approach to KAL

Any phrase can be used as the starting point for a rap. The following was suggested by a Year 2 child around Christmas time:

'Sometimes it's cold at Christmas time.'

The children, working in a group at the computer screen, developed this by adding further 'sometimes' ideas.

'Sometimes we wear our gloves in the snow.'
'Sometimes we put on our coats to play.'

And then they stumbled upon something which *always* happened, having presents. So the rap concluded with some 'always' lines.

'Always we have presents at Christmas.'
'Always we're very happy at Xmas.'

The children worked with an electric keyboard rhythm on in the background, and had to fit four beats into each line. With more experienced composers the metrical restraint could be tightened by asking for alliteration and/or rhyme, or for 'like' lines involving comparisons, and so on.

To do this the children need to draw on intuitive understanding of English rhythm, how the stress usually falls on content words;[14] and an understanding of textual pattern, that is, using the repetitive 'sometimes' plus an example, which changes to 'always' for a clinching end.

These aspects of the process of composition were discussed among the children and with the teacher prompting and typing but not directing. They used the term 'beat' as a handy term which they knew already, but not as applied to language, and drew on their knowledge of the parallelism and reiteration common in popular songs.

But these aesthetic pattern-making features also have applications for the development of language skills. They provide a model of one kind of textual coherence, and when they had the printout, the text could be used as a reading text with a good deal of supportive repetition. Since the children had constructed the text, they could use this knowledge as the basis for reading strategies.

Poems, especially raps, are particularly good texts for developing early literacy because they require imagination to make and to interpret; they are conveniently short to be worked or thought over at leisure, and they are usefully reiterative, and give scope for the children to develop reading strategies based on grammatical predictability. They read:

1 In the process of drafting and editing at the screen.
2 In the process of reading and illustrating the printout.

3   In the process of rehearsing for a full performance with the microphone and tape-recorder.
4   In the process of amalgamating different versions.
5   In the process of preparing a finished cassette sleeve/programme.

Reading and spelling

Both reading and spelling can be looked at aesthetically as interesting processes in themselves, rather than as goals to be rushed towards, or as material presented so that what the children do is either right or wrong. Recent research suggests that children are more likely to master spelling if they are relaxed and free to experiment at first with their own spellings, and interpretations of writing, without the teacher being over-anxious to push them immediately into right and wrong categories.[15] Children's spellings can be extremely creative and insightful as to the true phonetic structures of words, which are often not shown by the orthodox spellings.[16]

Just as in maths children begin by using non-standard methods of measuring things, so that they get a conception of measuring as such, so too in the early stages of spellings they can be encouraged to show a similar resourcefulness and begin working out in practical terms how the spelling system works through taking it on and trying to make their own.

3.5 The process of spelling

1   Comment on what aspects of the English spelling system the children seem to have grasped, or begun to grasp in the following quotations.

   a   *Four-year-old*
   Hw r you wan you gad i chans sand is ol i ladr Rad r you taceg car iv yorsalf
   b   *Five-year-old*
   Dot mak noys my dadday wrx hir this si wer me dadaa wrx b cwiyit

(Both quotations from *Children's Creative Spelling* (1986) by Charles Read. London: Routledge and Kegan Paul.)

2   **Assessment**
   a   What teaching strategies have been employed to obtain this kind of work?
   b   Which statements of attainment in *English in the National Curriculum*, Attainment Target 4, have been approached?

Reading can be taught in a similar way, giving scope to the children's experiment, and allowing them to work with what book or other text they find attractive, at first inventing the wording for themselves, doing play reading, joining in with an adult while the adult reads aloud, and so on. Work on phonics can be begun orally by drawing children's attention to the component sound words, through raps, rhymes, games with alliteration and so on.[17]

Cultural and aesthetic function

The two kinds of justification for teaching KAL in primary schools overlap. For example, if we work on the comparison of two or more dialects of English, let us say the non-standard speech of the Black Country and standard English, we shall have to work both at the level of words, sounds and sentence structures, and at the level of class and culture.

3.6 An accent and dialect notebook

1 KAL as fact
The children keep a loose-leaf folder in which they have sections on the accents and dialects they hear on television soaps such as *Neighbours*, *EastEnders*, *Bread*, *Coronation Street*, *The News*, and so on, and on accents and dialects of members of the class.

2 They also make lists of contrasts with improvised spellings such as:

'You'm coming' (Yaum koomeengg) (Black Country)
'You're coming' (Yor kumming) (SE)

3 Extension
The children do tapes in which they imitate the speech of particular members of the class or soaps in:
    a specially composed poems or stories related to a particular area of Britain or an English speaking country;
    b versions of soaps in which the region is deliberately altered.

4 Assessment
    a Make two lists, one of aspects of this work which relate to the level of culture, and one of aspects relating to the details of language.
    b Cite aspects of the work, or how you might develop it, which entail KAL and are justifiable on:
        i aesthetic (and enabling) grounds;
        ii cultural grounds.

Notes

1 Henry Widdowson's Appendix to the Kingman Report sets out a particularly important area of difficulty, which the subsequent Cox Reports and ENC have still not addressed: exactly how KAL may enhance writing skills.

2 Second Cox Report: 6.6.

3 The idea that the 'subject' is largely shaped by language has received a great deal of attention by writers in the Lacanian post-structuralist school. A good English exploration of the idea can be found in *Language and Materialism* (1977) by Rosaline Coward and John Ellis (London: Routledge and Kegan Paul).

4 See also *English in the National Curriculum*, Attainment Target 2, level 5(e) on the difference between fact and opinion.

5 The area has been very intensely studied since the 1960s. A good introduction is provided in *Studies in the Theory of Ideology* (1984) by John B. Thompson (Cambridge: Polity Press). See also *Structuralism and Semiotics* (1977) by Terence Hawkes (London: Methuen). A background to the particular approach adopted in this book can be found in *Introducing Stylistics* (1989) by John Haynes (London: Unwin Hyman). For a point of view angled towards literature, see *Structuralist Poetics* (1975) by Jonathan Culler (London: Routledge). Other names to look out for are Roland Barthes, Michel Foucault, Michel Pecheux, Colin McCabe, Julia Kristeva, Terry Eagleton, Gunther Kress.

6 See *Accent Dialect and the School* (1975) by Peter Trudgill (London: Edward Arnold).

7 See *Language as Ideology* (1969) by Gunther Kress and Robert Hodge (London: Routledge) and *Language and Control* (1979) by Roger Fowler, Bob Hodge, Gunther Kress and Tony Trew (London: Routledge).

8 Jacques Derrida is a radical left French writer whose most well known book is *Of Grammatology* (1986) (Baltimore: Johns Hopkins University Press) translated by Gayatri Chakravorty Spivak. Derrida makes claims which unsettle traditional notions of the role of language in society, and about the status usually accorded to written language as opposed to speech.

9 Cox Report (1989), 6.6.

10 'Plenty to Cheer, but . . .' by Henrietta Dombey in *Times Educational Supplement*, 13 May, 1988.

11 'The Difficulty of Grammar' by W. J. Macauley in *British Journal of Educational Psychology*, **17** (1947). *An Experimental Enquiry into the Functions and Value of Formal Grammar in the Teaching of English, with Special Reference to the Teaching of Correct Written English in children aged 12–14*, (1962) unpublished Ph D thesis by R. J. Harris, London: Institute of Education.

12 See 'Attitudes to Language and Language Teaching' (1979) by W. Harpin in *English in Education*, **13**, 2; *Attitudes to English Usage* (1970) by W. H. Mittins, M. Salu, M. Edminson and S. Coyne (London: OUP).

13 There has, however, been a good deal of debate as to whether the overall impact of Cox does not, in fact, make standard English appear superior. See, for example, H. Rosen (1990). The dangers of using the term 'appropriate', however, were seen by Peter Trudgill some time ago:
    . . . some colleges of education have now begun to argue that although, say, standard English is no more 'correct' than other varieties it is nevertheless 'appropriate' to certain situations and should be taught for that reason. 'Appropriateness' can easily become simply 'correctness' under another name, and our view is that this approach should be treated with caution. *On Dialect* (1983) by Peter Trudgill (Oxford: Basil Blackwell, p. 205).

14 That is, words which can easily be described or represented in a drawing as opposed to 'function words' such as 'the', and 'is', 'me', which cannot.

15 Also in practice. A Birmingham teacher who switched from the typical spelling book and told children to work out their own spellings when they did stories, writes: 'What has surprised me most is that this approach has actually led to a marked improvement in the spellings within the children's writing.' 'Curriculum Initiatives' in *About Writing: the SCDC National Writing Project Newsletter*, n6, Summer 1987.

16 Essential reading on the imaginative approach to spelling is *Children's Creative Spelling* (1986) by Charles Read (London: Routledge).

17 See Chapter 8 for fuller comments on the KAL element in the teaching of early literacy.

PART TWO

Text, context and classroom

Part Two is devoted to providing a working model of language in use, that is of texts. This provides a framework within which all aspects of KAL can be considered. Chapter 4 outlines the model; Chapter 5 indicates how it can be used to see where KAL arises, and how it can be made to arise.

The orientation of this Part, then, is towards the teacher's own KAL. But this is not sharply to be distinguished from KAL the children develop. Rather a joint kind of learning is assumed. The teacher not only helps the children to find and develop the KAL they already have; in doing this the teacher develops his/her own KAL.

4 | *A working model*

Knowledge about knowledge about language

To foster KAL among children, teachers need not have a detailed knowledge of linguistics; but they do need to have a broad model of language, to allow them to see where particular insights on the part of children may lead, and hence which of them is worth following up. In this chapter such a model will be outlined and then some suggestions will be made about its use.

Texts

We will think in terms of texts rather than language as such. Language is a very wide resource from which we draw when we actually speak or write. Actually speaking or writing is always done in a text. Examples of texts are a conversation with the bus driver, a letter from a friend, a notice saying 'Keep off the grass', a poem, a telephone conversation. Texts may be of any length from one word like 'Stop' to an epic or a holy book. There are occasions when the beginning and ending of a text are difficult to assess, but in practical everyday life the limits of a text are seldom a problem.[1]

We can usually identify where it starts and stops and detect an overall unity. Often this coincides with some physical boundary. A novel is contained in its covers, a notice in its big piece of wood or card. A telephone conversation is bounded by picking up and putting down the receiver, a conversation by the length of time the people stand at the garden fence, and so on.

Texts have a unity but this is not directly connected to the grammar of the sentences that make them up. The unity of a text is a unity of meaning, not of grammar. So to understand how a text works we need to look at the kinds of meaning it conveys. Meaning is, of course, carried by words in grammatical orderings, but its relation to grammatical rules is an indirect one. In studying texts we are interested in grammar and vocabulary more as carriers of meaning than as abstract rules.

A school day can be thought of as a succession of different texts. The children arrive at school and have conversations with each other. Then, perhaps the register is read. They may then look at a story book, or have a debate, or draw a picture. Texts may interrupt one another. During the reading of the register, the school secretary may come in with a telephone message about someone's dental appointment. The reading of the register stops for a moment, the secretary's message intervenes, then the reading of the register resumes.

It should be remembered that the term 'text' is used to refer to spoken as well as written exchanges, and that ordinary conversations, though they may appear unorganised, have their own structures, just as a nursery rhyme or a mathematical calculation does.

4.1 This morning's texts

1 Make a list of the first ten texts you have been engaged with this morning. Include spoken as well as written texts, and such texts as signs, greetings, and notices.

2 Make diagrams, or a single complex diagram, to show
   a The sequence of the texts.
   b What marked the beginnings and ends of them.
   c What the purpose of each was, for example:
      i action ('Keep off the grass');
      ii information ('High Street');
      iii interaction (conversation beginning 'Morning, darling . . .';
      iv contact (telephone call to a parent whose child has not arrived for school);
      v entertainment (*Beano* story).

3 All these texts form a kind of narrative of your early morning.
   a What is it that makes the narrative coherent?
   b How are the texts connected to each other?

4.2 A telephone call

Half of a conversation

1 Working with a partner take turns to make a telephone call. The person not making the call tape-records your half of the call only. Then the roles are reversed.

2 Transcribe the half-conversations, or at least five minutes of each, setting them out like a play with the turns of the person at the other end of the line left blank.

3 Each partner then reconstructs the blank turns of the conversation they have not been engaged in.

4 Make a list of:
   a The *textual* clues you used.
   b The *contextual* clues you used.

5 Rewrite the telephone conversation as if it were a face-to-face conversation, and list in two columns words and phrases which are peculiar to each.

6 Imagine you had to explain what was going on on the tape to someone from a society in which there were no telephones.

The word 'hello', then, has a particular usage in telephone calls. And this is because telephone calls are the kind of 'blind' texts they are. The context in which a text functions can be looked at in the very wide perspective of the culture which has produced it,[2] in the context of business life, and in a more immediate individual way. Here, in the more immediate perspective it is useful to distinguish four components, or influences on how the text functions:

1 The medium of communication.
2 The content.
3 The interactions of the people involved.
4 The setting.[3]

These can also be illustrated from the comic strip picture shown in Figure 4.1.

Figure 4.1 *Text and context of situation*
(Source: 'TV Centre' in Fast Forward, *BBC Magazines, 1–7 August, 1990, p.12)*

Setting

If, for the moment, we imagine that the strip is not fictional, but 'real', then the words in the speech bubbles being spoken by the DJ form a part of the text. Everything else in the picture represents the immediate setting – the radio studio. The wider setting is what the DJ will be aware of but not in a direct or fully conscious way. This is indicated by the caption at the top: 'It's Sunday afternoon and Bruno Brookes is doing his chart show.' Wider still, as the typical reader of the strip will know, is that this is set in Australia, and connected to the soap opera *Neighbours*, in which a number of pop stars act, Craig McLachlan being one of them. Wider still is the setting of the context of culture, that is the portrayal of Australian life styles, soap operas, and the pop and youth sub-culture, with which primary school children of a surprisingly young age identify. This is also a technologically developed culture, and international.

Interaction

When people have a conversation they do not just utter words; speech is always action. They produce 'speech acts'. When Bruno talks he is also performing the acts of informing, joking, promoting, describing, announcing, and so on. In doing so he interacts with his audience, and even though they cannot immediately reply to what he says, as they might in a face-to-face conversation, he tries as far as possible to talk as if he were face-to-face and chatting. His attitude to his audience is friendly and casual but at the same time he has a certain control over them because they have to listen to whatever track he puts on, and because he, as a professional radio DJ, has a high social status, and the influence of an expert on the charts and the performers.

The interactive aspect of the context, then, is in part what Bruno does in and through speaking, and in part his overall attitude and emotional impact, the atmosphere he creates which makes his listeners like him personally and interested in what he has to say and play.

4.3 Text, context, wider context, culture

1 Taking the *TV Centre* strip for the moment as a 'real' situation, make a note of the clues given in the picture as to the immediate setting in which the speech bubbles are spoken.

2 List the texts which Jason himself is involved in as he cooks. How does the kitchen setting affect what is said in the bubbles? Another way of looking at this is to ask why the writer chose to represent Jason in that particular setting. Can we say the setting itself expresses a meaning of a kind?

3 What is the context of culture of the frame? How is it expressed in the pictures? How does it affect Jason's words?

Medium

The medium of communication in the studio is oral language, of course, but augmented by the radio microphone. This affects interaction because, except for moments when he might take a telephone call from a listener, the communication is one-way, and because it assumes that Bruno's communication is not directed to any particular person. And the medium also affects the setting in the sense that, if there is to be a radio programme, then a purpose-built setting is required, the radio studio with its equipment.

Bruno speaks spontaneously. He is not reading from a script, and his words give way from time to time to the music he is playing, the songs making up separate texts. Since this is spoken (and sung) language rather than written, it depends on time, that is, once the words have been uttered they are gone, whereas in a book, if someone has missed something, the pages can be turned back, and the text re-read at any time. Speech can, of course, be recorded, but still, while the words are being listened to, they move through time. The page is fixed and still.

4.4 Drawing a cheque

1 Before you next go to the bank to draw a cheque devise a dialogue in which you attempt to predict what will be said.

2 After having gone, describe the interactions you engage in when you draw a cheque. Look at these from the point of view of:
    a how purpose affects text;
    b what is done in and through language, for example 'greeting', 'requesting' etc. (speech acts); and
    c the expression of formality, politeness, etc.

3 Consider face-to-face and wider roles and institutions.
    a Yourself and the bank clerk as a representative of the bank.
    b Yourself and the bank clerk as an individual.
    c Yourself and the bank through the cheque itself.
    d Where and how you have freedom to control or vary the interaction.
    e The ways in which the bank's lack of confidence in customers' honesty is present but not expressed.

Content

A text also usually conveys something besides the personality and attitudes of the speakers, though different types of texts vary according to how far they aim to inform or how far they aim to charm, insult, intimidate and so on. The content of a text may be a part of the setting, as when Bruno refers to a disk or tape which he has in his hands, or to the heat in the studio, or it may be something remote from the studio, the recording artist, Craig McLachlan, for example, or a completely imaginary place.

Content may be immediately embedded in the setting, then, or remote from the setting. It may be physical (a disk) or it may be abstract, that is other texts. Bruno may refer to the disk as a physical object, or he may refer to it as another text with its own content, interactions and medium, a text within a text. The relationship between content and setting is important in teaching, since too remote a relation tends to be difficult for children to relate to, especially infants.

Genre

In Figure 4.2 we set out four ways in which the context affects a text: the medium to be used, the interactions involved, the content to be conveyed, and the setting in which the text functions. The particular way in which these components of a text are mixed is the 'genre' of the text.[4] As a shorthand to underline this we will use the acronym MICS for the 'mix' of medium, interaction, content and setting in a text.

Genres become institutionalised, and so they arouse expectations. For example, we can guess that a gas bill will be in a printed medium, received through the post, and that it will constitute an impersonal interaction where the gas authority makes demands and mentions sums of money we have to pay. A story on the other hand may be either written or spoken, but we can be sure that it will assign us, the audience, a relatively passive listening role and will have, as its contents, real or imaginary actions of some kind. Generally speaking (but by no means always) the interactive facet is the easiest to predict, that is, what the participants or user/creators of the text will do.

4.5 Menu and recipe

1 Find or devise a menu item and a recipe for the same dish.

2 Make a chart showing:
  a The MICS components of each.
  b The main differences between the texts from the points of view of:
    i   grammar;
    ii   vocabulary;
    iii interaction between writer and reader;
    iv   setting.
  c What they have in common.

The particular mix of components reflects the purpose the user/creator of a text has. Thus, genre can be regarded as the imprint on the text of its purpose. A simplified diagram of the relation between text and context is given in Figure 4.2.

Figure 4.2 *Text and context*

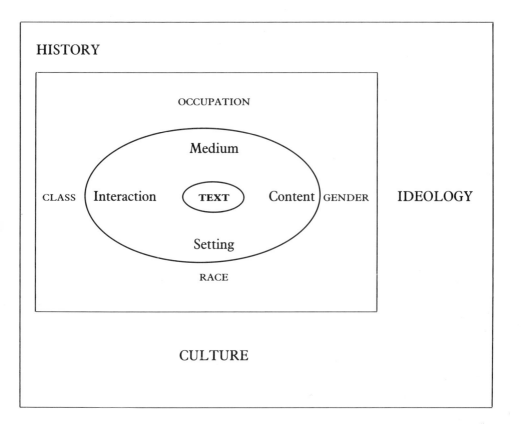

Context of situation and the National Curriculum

ENC emphasises that language be taught in relation to its context. This means looking at how the text is affected by its setting, who is speaking and who is being spoken to about what, and by the medium. The details of speech or writing can be made sense of best, not by looking just at the way individual sentences are constructed, but by seeing how they fit into their context of situation, and what purposes they serve for an individual or for the society. Bruno's broadcast text can be seen as fulfilling the purposes of entertainment, and commerce. At the individual level, the text has the purpose of projecting Bruno's personality and informing listeners about the latest situation in the charts.

ENC emphasises this approach to texts, that is looking at language according to its purpose, as opposed to the traditional approach in which the details of the wording were studied in isolation. But the assumption behind much of ENC is that the detailed verbal structure in a text are as they are because they have to serve the general functions of communicating a content in a setting, and interacting through a medium.

Medium, it must be recalled, is the criterion taken by Cox and ENC for breaking up the curriculum into three profile components. The first is devoted to spoken language, and the other two to written language. This primary division is shown in Figure 4.3. Within these primary divisions in ENC the attainment targets are broken down on the basis of interactions, primarily whether the communication is passive (listening, reading) or active (speaking, writing, handwriting, spelling).

Figure 4.3 *Profile components: medium and interaction*

	ORAL MEDIUM	WRITTEN MEDIUM
PASSIVE INTERACTION	Profile Component 1 AT 1: listening	Profile Component 2 AT 2: reading
ACTIVE INTERACTION	speaking	Profile Component 3 AT 3: writing AT 4: spelling AT 5: handwriting AT 4/5: presentation

Within this framework other subdivisions are made in relation to setting, in particular settings in which standard English is appropriate, and settings in which a non-standard dialect is used. From the point of view of KAL, the teacher needs to manage the classroom so that it becomes a setting for activities which put children into a position where KAL must arise. And to do this all four text components must be taken into account.

Conclusion

The model of the relations between texts and context sketched in this chapter is, of course, one kind of KAL, a kind of KAL appropriate to teachers. We turn in the next chapter to see how this model can be used to facilitate children's own development of KAL.

Notes

1 For example, is one volume of *Encylopaedia Britannica* a text, or do all the volumes together make a text? Or is each article a text? And, in principle, a serial programme like *The Archers* has a beginning but no end.
2 'Culture' is a vague word, and it is used here in the most general sense. It could refer to the person's membership of a teenage society or movement, to class, to ethnic background, even to gender, or to nation.

3 This way of looking at the context of situation is derived from M. A. K. Halliday's conception of register – see *Language as Social Semiotic* (1978) London: Edward Arnold. I have adapted the terms 'field', 'tenor' and 'mode' to the more self-explanatory 'setting/content', 'interaction', and 'medium'.

4 In any actual text, of course, the components are synthesised and it is not possible to isolate and give boundaries to each component. The 'MICS' components provide an analytical tool based on the idea of linguistic 'functions'. Any particular piece of text will typically fulfil a number of functions simultaneously. Analytically it can be looked at from the point of view of any one of them.

5 | Texts in which knowledge about language is developed

KAL themes

Figure 4.3 in Chapter 4 gives a sketch of the overall structure of ENC. Within this structure a number of broad themes are mentioned. These too can be studied within the MICS framework. They are summarised in Figure 5.1. It must be borne in mind that Figure 5.1 is intended to cover all attainment targets at all levels in Key Stages 1 and 2;[1] that is, it includes work on early reading, writing and spelling in the infant school.

Figure 5.1 *KAL themes*

G	MEDIUM	Difference between speech and writing Appropriateness to type of communication
E	INTERACTION	Appropriateness of text to purpose and audience
N	CONTENT	Appropriateness of text to factual or imaginary content
R		
E	SETTING	Appropriateness of text to setting Differences among dialects and languages

General relationship between KAL and classroom texts

KAL may arise in the context of everyday work in the following ways (among others).

(a) Devising texts collaboratively
When children are devising a text collaboratively, and have to talk about how it ought to go, what ought to be where, what their aims are, what the layout and wording should be, and so on.

(b) Turning texts back upon themselves
When texts can be turned back upon themselves, as in debates and one speaker

may refer to someone else's words earlier in the same text, perhaps to point out an inconsistency or to sum up.

(c) Composing to specifications
Where children write a text to specifications: a fixed number of words, or sentences, or number of lines or a metre.

(d) Collaborative reviewing of texts
When a written or recorded text is subject to collaborative editing, or rehearsal for a performance.

(e) Collaborative inference drawing
Where a text requires interpretation and has to be scrutinised closely. Examples are riddles and jokes, or activities involving the interpretations of codes. And of course, some literary texts.

(f) Collaborative preparation of a presentation
Such as a poster, where discussion occurs as to what should be pasted where, with what kinds of lettering, spelling, layout, and so on.

In thinking about texts which naturally give rise to KAL, whether or not the children go on to set out *what* that knowledge is in an explicit way, all four text components/facets must be taken into account.

Texts in which KAL occurs, then, are all texts in which language and textuality themselves are made the content of talking or writing. The basic strategy in teaching KAL is to motivate children so that they think that talking about a particular piece of language has some point and interest. This is set out in schematic form in Figure 5.2. The categories here are not discrete.

Figure 5.2 *Kinds of text enabling KAL*

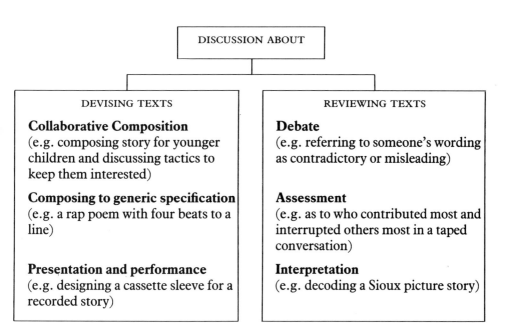

A great deal of text-making requires ongoing reflection about how things have gone so far, and a number of the activities could be applied to a single text.

5.1 Finding the KAL-text

1 Rapping
Children compose a rap poem orally. They use an electronic keyboard to keep a steady rhythm, and record versions on a tape-recorder. They then make a script together, based on all their contributions and photocopy this, then reduce it in size so that it can go inside the cassette container, together with a photograph of the group, its name, and a list of their roles in the production.

2 KAL-texts
Make an analysis with a diagram to show the relation between two KAL-texts, and two content-texts here.

3 Curriculum
What justification is there for this activity from the point of view of:
  a Development of early literacy?
  b Later education in literature?
  c Multicultural awareness?

The constant factor in Figure 5.2 is conversation. For the children to think about language they need to talk to each other. This implies that the fundamental KAL text is going to be conversation, counting debate and similar texts such as interviews as variant forms of conversation. The other texts mentioned are the topics of conversations. So, looked at in this way, all KAL comes down to is making the texts, or parts of them, the content of conversation. The conversations are either prospective (devising something to be said) or retrospective (reviewing something already said) including texts which review and devise texts as they are going on, like debates or rehearsals. The text which the children, or teachers, use as a lens through which to look into other texts, or other parts of the same text, we will call a *KAL-text*. Since the text being looked into forms the content of the KAL text, this will be referred to as the *content-text* where it is necessary to distinguish. Figure 5.3 shows the relation between the KAL-text and the content-text, that is, the poem being prepared.

Figure 5.3   *KAL-text and content-text (rap poem)*

KAL-TEXT: DISCUSSION		
MEDIUM INTERACTION	CONTENT	SETTING
speech listening together and informal turn-taking on task	wording, rhythm, performance of	classroom or quiet area, junction box and head phones

Inner table (RAP POEM):

MEDIUM	INTERACTION	CONTENT	SETTING
spoken	unscripted rehearsal for	'I'm	recording
electronic	comments of group	glidin'	studio in
keyboard	performance to class	in my	store room
rhythm		dream of	
on tape		you . . .'	
		etc.	

5.2 KAL and poetry

1 Poetry as a genre

Poetry is a genre in which one (distinctive) purpose is drawing the reader's attention to processes by which the poem was composed, and writing poetry requires self-conscious awareness of rhythm, the sounds that make up words, the choice of words, and so on. Often poems are composed to a framework such as a metre or rhyme scheme, or parallelism.

2 KAL as process

Choose a particular poem, and list the aspects of compositional process you needed to notice to read it properly as a poem and not some other kind of text.

3 Poem as content-text

What KAL texts would be involved in the work of preparing and rehearsing a performance of the poem for a video film, working with a director, and a camera man?

KAL and MICS

A good way to approach KAL is to break down a text into its MICS components. Imagine children are devising a poster to inform the rest of the school that there

Figure 5.4 *MICS for poster announcing exhibition*

Medium

Writing, or rather calligraphy. Particular attention needs to be given to lettering style and size, and the spacing out of words and other materials on the card.

Interaction

Public, addressed to anyone who is interested rather than specific individuals, though the main audience is likely to be other children in the school. The notice must also be attention-gaining and produce a sense of friendly encouragement to come, and should take account of younger children.

Content

Glider exhibition, time, place etc. Attention is needed to the exact choice of words, especially in the title. This overlaps with the interactional component, showing the exhibition in its best light. Content also interacts with medium because the amount of content to be included is limited by spatial design.

Setting

School hall, corridors, classrooms. Here it is closely related to content since the setting of the exhibition must be mentioned as part of the content. Also the school setting is shared by others, which reduces the amount of information to be provided since other children will not need detailed instructions as to where Class 10 is.

will be an exhibition of model gliders one afternoon. The teacher's planning begins with his or her reviewing MICS for this particular genre, the poster. A suggested review of this kind is given in Figure 5.4. Setting the components out, however impressionistically, is a useful way of checking that all possible ways into KAL are thought about. The main point of such a review is to see what the purpose of the poster is, and how the different MICS must function in it to fulfil that purpose.

KAL-text and classroom context

The key to KAL work, then, lies in the selection of KAL- and content-texts which, on the one hand the children find interesting, and on the other are justifiable educationally.

5.3 KAL and statements of attainment

1   Take any one strand at the same level across the ATs 2–5, and look at the examples suggested in the right-hand column.

2   Sketch a short programme of work in which you adapt the examples to work which entails KAL. Relate these to strands at the same level in AT 1, which form the KAL texts.

3   For each KAL-text make a note as to whether it is devising, or reviewing.

Since KAL texts will generally involve face-to-face discussion, the classroom context must be one in which this sort of text can be produced. This may require some thought since it seems that most teachers still do very little oral work.[2] KAL texts can only be operated if the children have had some experience, or are working on acquiring skills, in group discussion. Developing the ability to turn-take, listen to others, respond, initiate further stretches of conversation should, of course, form a priority in infant, or even nursery, education. Simply asking a group to 'talk about' a tape or book, or 'discuss' a topic, can never be effective unless the children understand what the discourse conventions are, how they are supposed to behave, *and* have had some practice in them.

Knowledge of conversational conventions is itself KAL. And it sometimes has to be made explicit, for example, when a discussion breaks down. Children have to learn how to handle turn taking, not to interrupt, to challenge in a polite way, to apologise for a misunderstanding, and so on. Hence KAL is closely associated with oracy and AT 1.

Developing conversation

Conversation is the fundamental text. This is the one every human being masters, and the one that is used most frequently by all of us everyday. And conversations, like all texts, turn out to be as they are because of what the people concerned are doing, on the basis of the context of situation. Why are they talking? What have they 'got to say'?

One of the most suspect features of traditional teaching has been its suppression of talking. Where there is talk, overwhelmingly it is the teacher who talks and the children who listen.[3] The classroom is dominated by the written word which, of course, can be studied in solitude and silence. Nowadays, the value of conversation, including conversations about reading and writing have become widely recognised.[4]

5.4 Researching conversation

1 Taping
Tape-record a conversation among children when they are working in groups or, if the recorder is good enough, while they are having school dinner.

2 Listening
Get permission from the participants in the conversation, and give the tape to a group to listen to with headphones. The children have a set of cards asking them to assess:
  a   how many times each person speaks;
  b   who has the longest turn;
  c   who interrupts the most;
  d   who is rude most;
  e   who asks the most questions; and
  f   who gives the most information to the others.

3 Imitating
Using simple stick drawings do a series of comic strip frames imitating typical roles, phrases, and postures of the conversants, using 'ums' and 'ers', self-corrections and so on to make it 'sound like talk and not writing'.

4 Justification
What kind of justification would you give this work?
  a   as KAL;
  b   in terms of ENC;
  c   in terms of later work to which it leads.

Developing conversational skills requires KAL on the part of the teacher, in particular the recognition that if children are to converse then they must have something 'real' to talk about, something which they *can* talk about naturally, so that they can see the value of following rules for taking turns and managing disagreement. Figure 5.5 is a representation of a KAL-text for discussing the poster summarised in Figure 5.4. In other words Figure 5.4 shows the content-text of Figure 5.5.

From the point of view of the development of conversational skills, it is the interactional component that requires closest attention. The children have to learn to interact by taking conversational turns without interruptions or shoutings down. To reduce the possibility of this, attention needs to be given to the interactive

Figure 5.5 *KAL-text about poster-making*

MEDIUM	INTERACTION	CONTENT (TEXT)	SETTING
speech and pointing	turn-taking advising hypothesising demonstrating offering	text of poster in process including writing materials, card paints, etc.	classroom with focus on items under 'content'
	speech roles		members' areas of responsibility

context, and the members of the group given, at the outset, specific conversational roles related to specific areas of responsibility in the work being discussed. It is essential for teachers to familiarise children with the rituals of the meeting and with the roles of the chair, secretary, members with particular briefs, and so on. This ritual can also be the basis of less formal but still task-directed conversation.

5.5 A meeting

1 Setting

Draw a sketch of where children are to sit to hold a meeting to discuss the design and content of a poster to exhibit their work in gliders and gliding.

2 Interaction

Make notes on how you would organise:

a *Roles* – There should be a chair, a secretary and members with special responsibility for specific aspects of the content or design.

b *Rituals* – There should be a formal method of:

i ensuring that the chair controls who speaks and that everyone knows who has the right to hold the floor; and

ii verbal formulas for expressing disagreement.

3 Content

Make a note of other documents, pictures, models etc., which would be needed as content-texts, including an agenda, how the meeting will be timed to cover everything, how a record of it is to be kept and agreed.

4 Initiation

Indicate how the classroom would be organised so that a group could be initiated into meeting conventions.

Conclusion

In this chapter we have looked at the way in which KAL is studied as a part of ongoing classwork. This involves two types of text, one being studied and the other being used to study it. In setting up KAL in the classroom the teacher sets up a classroom context which ensures that text devising, text reviewing, performance/rehearsal do in fact take place. This entails looking into the four MICS components of a text.

The MICS components are related to the structure of ENC, and in Part Three we look at the most important themes in ENC as far as KAL is concerned, the distinction between speaking and writing, and the sensitivity of a text to its context. The distinction between speaking and writing is a matter of medium, while appropriateness relates to the overall mix of components, that is, to the genre.

Both Cox and ENC recommend that KAL be integrated into ongoing classwork, though there are times in ENC where KAL is treated in the manner of linguistics, especially in the *Non-Statutory Guidance*.[5] We have focused on the integrated approach.

Notes

1 'Opportunities for the development of children's knowledge about language exists in all Key Stages and all ATs' *ENC Non-statutory Guidance* (1990) London: National Curriculum Council, p. D7, section 2.3.
2 *Language Education* (1989) by Frances Christie (Oxford: Oxford University Press, p. 21).
3 The word 'talk' is used to describe any kind of spoken text and covers both speaking and listening.
4 This is usually linked with collaborative learning. See, for example, *The Meaning Makers* (1989) by Gordon Wells (London: Hodder and Stoughton), *Learning to Read* (1982) by Margaret Meek (London: Bodley Head), *Read it to me Now!* (1990) by Hilary Minns (London: Virago).
5 See pages D9 and D10, where both 'Names and Terms KS 1, 2' and 'The language of persuasion KS 4' show a transmissional model of teaching, at least at the level of planning. This kind of work on the facts of language can be done as a project on its own, of course, but it is not easily assimilable into other kinds of work.

PART THREE

Themes in knowledge about language

Part Three deals with the main themes addressed in KAL. These are treated in terms of, but not determined by, ENC. The KAL component of ENC is mainly compatible with the overall interpretation of KAL taken in this book.[1] Differences arise in three ways. The first is a matter of emphasis, the greater importance given here to KAL as the model of all language work in the primary school. The second is the relative lack of attention paid in these pages to KAL as linguistic facts. The third arises from the vagueness in the wording of ENC, which reflects its political origins.

6 | *Speech and writing*

Medium and the National Curriculum

In ENC the distinction between speech and writing is structural. It separates AT 1 from the other ATs. The theme also figures in particular strands across the ATs, for example in AT 2 L5(e) where children are expected to

'. . . show in discussion the ability to recognise variations in vocabulary according to purpose, topic and audience, *and whether the language is spoken or written.*' [author's italics]

Also, the very concept of KAL implies a distinction between speech and writing, since most KAL-texts are oral, and most content-texts written. Thus, knowledge about the ways in which speech and writing differ is crucial for the teacher from the point of view of planning programmes of work, and for the child as part of the curriculum.

Spoken text and written text[2]

The main differences between speech and writing can be summed up as follows: Speech is usually composed as the speaker goes along and so is presented to us as a process in which any tidying up forms part of the text. Writing is presented as a product which has been tidied up in a draft form which we do not see.

Written language evolved after spoken language, and played a part in making people conscious of language as such. Written language is, generally, used in different contexts from spoken, and for different purposes, mainly to overcome distance and space, to make texts permanent, and to allow greater reflection on ideas.

Spoken and written texts have different kinds of grammar, and we must avoid regarding spoken texts as incoherent or ungrammatical because they differ from written ones.[3] To bring out the main differences between spoken and written texts we will look at the openings of two texts. The first is a conversation in which a child is telling a group, made up of her brother and cousin, and their teacher, a story about a dream she has had. The second is a written version of the story, as edited by the same child, Mandeep, and her cousin, Sona, to make a written short story. Mandeep and Sona were in Year 2 at the time, and Harjeet in Year 1. For convenience, the spoken version of the story will be referred to as 'tale', and the written version as 'story'.

Tale (Mandeep's dream: spoken)

1 *Mandeep*   I was in the bed, and this – I had a dream about a fox, to coming near me and had green eyes flashing to me.

2	*J.H.*	Hmm!
3	*Mandeep*	And then I was frightened. I hold my sister's hand, so we can find the place where we can . . . And we saw this old man. Had this thing and looking everywhere (*gesture*).
4	*J.H.*	A camera?
5	*Mandeep*	Yeah. And a lady said, 'Ah, these are little children. You want to come with me?' And we found a place. She told us where's the place and we found it – forest. Was all this food in. Bananas, orange, and that. And some things to eat.
6	*Sona*	Chapati. Chapati. And Roti.
7	*Mandeep*	And then we, and then we found the place. We ran. So . . . And we locked we locked the door, and then we saw this big castle down by the hill, this big castle. And there was a horse. And these doors opened.
8	*J.H.*	Yeah?
9	*Mandeep*	And the horse can get right in . . .

Story (Mandeep's dream: written)

I was in the bed and I had a dream about a fox was coming near me. And it had green eyes flashing at me. And then I was frightened and held my sister's hand so we can find a place where we can stay. And we saw this old man holding this telescope and looking everywhere.

And a black lady (Kalima) said, 'Ah, these are little children. You want to come with me?' And we followed her. We went in this cave. It was really big and dark. She left us there. In this cave. We shouted and screamed but there wasn't any sign of anybody. Then we went outside and fell in a hole, and the hole leaded to this forest.

It had lots of fruit it, bananas, orange and pears. Then we ran and ran. Then we saw a castle. We saw the door open itself. It was misty and dark inside. And the horse went inside the castle.

6.1 Conversational interactions

1 Discuss the following passage from Tale with a partner or small group.

9	*Mandeep*	And the horse can get right in. And the castle was bi bigger than all this house.
10	*Harjit*	Bigger than this school.
11	*Mandeep*	And I er I saw this man talking through the sky.
12	*Harjit*	You know what?
13	*Mandeep*	And he was . . .
14	*Harjit*	I saw God's leg. In the sky.
15	*J.H.*	Did you?
16	*Harjit*	All black. It was bigger than this school.
17	*J.H.*	You did!
18	*Sona*	Sir, you know our God, it's really . . .
19	*Harjit*	You know God? He can turn into anything.

20 *Sona*   Sir? Sir, you know our God? He can change into anything. He can change into you, sir. He can change . . .

    J.H.   Into me!

2   How does this passage differ from the passage that comes immediately before it?

3   Go though each turn and make a brief note as to what the speaker is doing in speaking (their speech acts). Suggest what their purposes are each time.

4   Rewrite the passage in the form of a factual account of 'Our God' from the point of view of Sona, but in your own language.

6.2 The written version

1   When Mandeep and Sona edited the oral text (tale), what broad principles did they follow? Bear in mind:

  a   cutting;

  b   additions;

  c   connections.

2   What still needs to be done to make the text sound like a finished written story?

Spoken texts differ from each other, so we cannot claim that every oral text will be like this one. There is a range of oral genres, shaped by the contexts in which they are used. But we can, still, use this conversation as a starting point to illustrate some very general points about oral texts.

6.3 Oral texts

1   Make MICS analyses of two of the following oral texts (where you can, use an actual recording or transcription; or use your recollection of what was said):

  a   a popular song;

  b   a newscast on television;

  c   reading and responding to the class register list;

  d   ringing up and making a directory enquiry;

  e   a story or anecdote told during school assembly.

2   Note the main differences in the texts from the point of view of:

  a   the purposes of speakers and listeners;

  b   who speaks most and why;

  c   aspects of the wording which is ritualistic and/or very highly predictable.

Medium

Most oral texts are composed as the speakers go along. Mandeep cannot erase her spoken words and edit them. Her alterations are manifest. In her first turn, she begins to say 'and this', but stops and starts again with 'I had a dream about'. It looks as if she had wanted to mention the fox straight away, but then remembers that before that she must mention that the fox came in a dream, not into her bedroom.

The dash was put in as part of the teacher's transcription of the text from the tape-recording. It reminds us that speech is not punctuated. Nor are words separated or sentences shown. When speech is written down decisions have to be made based on intonation and grammar. And intonation can express shades of feeling and emphasis that are difficult to capture in writing.

Speech tends to be used for more casual interactions than writing, and reveals the person's accent. And dialect is far more common in speech than in writing. Mandeep is of Indian background but she speaks with a Black Country accent. It may be, too, that as English is her second language, this affects her grammar and vocabulary in places, fluent as she is.

Speaking allows her, also, to make use of facial expressions and gestures. Hence, in turn 3, she can say 'this thing' and refer to her own gesture.

There is a temptation to see spoken grammar as less finished than written. This is because, for generations, teachers have taken writing as the model of 'good grammar', and imagined that in speaking we should attempt to match writing. But, in fact, spoken and written texts have different kinds of grammar. We have referred to Mandeep's change of direction in her turn 1. We should not see this as a 'mistake', however. After all it makes perfectly good sense, and when she says 'this' it acts as an advanced warning that a key piece of information is in the offing.

Spoken language has more complex grammar than the written word in the sense that the sentences wind about more, and there is greater freedom to leave material unstated, for example, in structures like 'Was all this food in' (turn 5). In speech, the information is less tightly packed than in writing. This is shown by the larger number of function words in proportion to content words. Functional words are words like 'are', 'me', 'for', 'the', 'of', which are difficult to define in a dictionary.

6.4 Density of information

1 Compare the following passages – one spoken and one written.

X: Spoken

Mandeep	I was in the *bed* and this – I had a *dream about* a *fox*, to *coming near* me and had *green eyes flashing* to me.
Teacher	Hmmm!
Mandeep	And then I was *frightened*. I *hold* my *sister's hand*, so we can *find* the *place* where we can . . . And we *saw* this *old man*. Had this *thing* and *looking everywhere*.
Teacher	A *camera*?
Mandeep	Yeah. And a *lady said*, 'Ah, these are *little children*.'

Y: Written

I was in the *bed* and I had a *dream about* a *fox* was *coming near* me. And it had *green eyes flashing* to me. And then I was *frightened* and *held* my *sister's hand* so we can *find* a *place* where we can *stay*. And we *saw* this *old man holding* this *telescope* and *looking everywhere*.

2   The words emphasised are so-called 'content' words. They can have relatively straightforward dictionary definitions and express the content. The other words are 'function' words which express more general grammatical relations.[4] Make a chart showing:
   a   the total number of words in each passage;
   b   the number of content words in each;
   c   the percentage of content words in each.

3   The passages are too short to be reliable statistically, but the difference in density of content words, and hence density of content, is nevertheless symptomatic of typical differences between spoken and written texts. Suggest some reasons for them.

4   Rewrite passage Y in your own words attempting now to reduce the number of function words as drastically as you can. You may find that simply trying to condense meaning has this effect.

Expressions typical of speech often sound out of place when written down. And what teachers sometimes refer to as 'bad English' is often spoken, and often also dialectal English, put into a written genre.[5] A related feature of written language is that it uses grammatical metaphors. For example, it will express a process as a static entity. Thus, although (*a*) below might be spoken or written, (*b*) or (*c*) are typically written.

(*a*)   James Flip likes to go to the park and fly his kite.
(*b*)   James Flip is a keen park kite flyer.
(*c*)   Keen park kite flyer James Flip (27) . . .

In (*a*) what James likes, what James does, and what the kite does are all expressed by verbs; but not in (*b*) and (*c*) where they are 'nominalised'. Children tend not to use grammatical metaphor, even when writing, though they do, of course, use metaphors based on individual words.

Speech is generally spontaneous and passing. Writing is generally edited and is relatively permanent. However, some spoken texts are planned, and some written ones unplanned. Planned speech is generally also scripted, as in drama or on the television, at least in societies which no longer have a strong oral tradition. An example of an unplanned written text is a draft, or a note to the milkman.

6.5 Film scripting

1 Groups prepare a news programme for video. The sketch here is based on work with top juniors. It will need adapting according to the age and experience of the children, of course. They plan and set up:

    a a studio with desk, backdrop;
    b programme staff with:
        i 2 newsreaders;
        ii director;
        iii musical director/tape-recorder operator;
        iv video camera operator;
    c an outside unit with:
        i person to be interviewed;
        ii suitable setting such as office, gym etc.;
        iii interviewer;
        iv director.

2 The newsbroadcast must be exactly 5 minutes long.

3 The sequence of events in the programme is mapped on a story board with drawings of stick figures in frames (like television screens), together with:
    a notes of the length of the frame;
    b kind of camera shot;
    c setting and people to be shot;
    d who, verbally, does what (speech acts);
    e studio props needed (e.g. computer screen with 'Lyng School News' for start of programme);
    f music cues.

4 **a** Children's assessment.
        i The class as a whole watches each group's programme and makes constructive criticisms (which could be followed by editing if facilities are available).
        ii Review what had to be done to keep to the time.
        iii Review what sorts of questions were the most likely to give the interviewee the best scope for reply, and what interviewers have to do when no answers are forthcoming.
    b Teacher's assessment – In what ways does this kind of work enhance children's awareness of the speech and writing?
        i Differences between them?
        ii Relations between them in this genre?

Interaction

Almost all texts are interactional because almost all have an audience. And one goal of KAL is to lead children to understand this through their own experience of speaking and writing for actual audiences.[6]

Spoken texts are often jointly composed. In Tale, Mandeep dominates because she is telling a story. But the other conversants also play a part in constructing the text. The second turn shows the teacher encouraging her, for example, and in Turn 4 he asks for a clarification, which he cannot do when reading a story.

The written text is designed to be read by one person (at a time) when the composer is not present. Writing overcomes distance, both in space and in time, but in writing it is relatively harder to express attitudes and emotions, or to establish a rapport with an audience.

In Tale the speaker has instant responses from her listeners and they can adjust what she says and how she says it according to their reactions, their facial expressions and body language. A writer has to use imagination to guess how the audience is going to respond, and what they need to know to understand the story.

Written texts usually have one author, although that author will probably have shown drafts to friends and had advice. In school, children often work together on a text. Thus, although it sounds as if there is just one speaker, the 'I' mentioned in Story, it is jointly composed. But the collaboration does not show as it does in Tale. In other words, Tale exhibits the process through which it was composed, whereas Story presents just the finished product.

Spoken texts on the media are like written texts in that the listener, like the reader, cannot respond immediately, cannot ask for clarification or complain that what is being said (or written) is nonsense or unfair. This one-way flow is associated with the power of the media speaker. Unlike Mandeep, the newscaster cannot be interrupted by the audience. Media texts, of course, are usually scripted and/or rehearsed, and edited, and so do not show process so readily as ordinary spoken texts do. Conversely, media texts can be scripted so as to produce the illusion of process.

Content

Some spoken texts simply aim to create a pleasant atmosphere among speakers and have no particular content. They may wander from topic to topic in order to 'make conversation'. The content may be not much more than an excuse for interaction. We may talk about the weather as a way of indicating general friendliness. In courtship, although there may be a nominal content, it may be simply a vehicle to express charm or affection, or make the other person laugh. Tale is not like this, though. The narrative content is the point of it, although, later, in passages not quoted, there are interventions by Mandeep's brother which are aimed at drawing attention to himself as much as contributing to the story.

Written texts can be prepared before they are communicated or published. Words can be altered, and expressions calculated at leisure. Hence, written texts are a good vehicle for working out complex ideas, or for doing mathematical calculations. And they are good for expressing compact thought, for example like the thought in poems, or in scientific formulas. Written texts are more suitable for carefully considered ideas too, for example, contracts or police evidence. We can check the meaning before we sign documents, and they stand as a permanent record afterwards.

Setting

Texts which are recorded, either by writing or in the electronic media, allow people in different immediate settings in space and time to communicate. Most written and oral media texts are also edited. And because the receiver and maker of such texts are in different places, such texts must be explicit about setting. Television, of course, provides the setting through pictures, though it is still usually necessary for the setting shown also to be explained verbally: 'I'm talking to you from the centre of Coventry . . .'

The writer cannot say 'this' or 'now' or 'him' without first explaining what they are referring to, or unless an illustration is provided, and even then exactly what is being referred to in the illustration must be made clear. Often the immediate setting of the writer, such as his study, is not directly relevant to the text.

Spoken texts like Tale are face-to-face, but still the teller must explain the setting of the story because it is different from that in which the teller and audience find themselves. But with some spoken texts, the setting is part of the content. Then, when the speaker and listener are in the same setting it is often not made explicit. Words like 'it', 'that', 'there' and 'you' tend to be used because what they refer to is obvious to the speakers, and can be clarified by gestures.

6.6 Embedded texts and speech

1 Rewrite Story as if you were telling their story orally and had a very detailed picture to which you continually refer. You are now not allowed to mention people or things referred to explicitly. You must say 'that', or 'in there' or 'her' or 'did that' etc., wherever you possible can.

2 Pass your version to someone else who has not read Story, and ask them to devise their own explicit version.

3 Make a note of all the words and phrases you have used as replacements for content words in Story. What do they have in common?

4 Make a note of all the embedded texts you make use of in your class. An embedded text is one in which the setting is visible to the speaker, and can be pointed to and referred to i.e. 'this', 'that', 'him' etc., because they are visible. Do the embedded texts have anything in common?

5 Devise a classroom activity in which children do 1 and 2 above at their own level and relate it to other classwork.

When children are learning to read they are helped by having the texts embedded in an immediate setting. That is why cornflakes packets, labels, street signs, and so on are such good early reading texts. When we read stories the setting of the story is often illustrated and so provides a similar kind of support. When writing, children start with a setting they have in mind and then have to find the written words. In reading, they start with the written words and have to find the setting. These are quite different processes.

A final point to make about setting is that writing and speech are sometimes particularly associated with particular settings. Some settings such as offices and studies are specially constructed with writing in mind; others, like radio studios and theatres, with planned speech in mind. Ordinary conversation has no special place, though it is sometimes forbidden as in libraries and at times in classrooms. The pub, perhaps, is purpose-built for conversation.

Comparing Tale and Story

These two texts were produced as part of a short project in which children were learning about the genre of story telling. First they had to understand how the audience is involved in the genre, even when silent. Then they had to see how a written story differed from a spoken conversational one. The work thus focused on both medium and interaction.

The main differences between Tale and Story are set out in Figure 6.1.

Figure 6.1 *Differences between Tale and Story*

G E N R E		MEDIUM	INTERACTION	CONTENT	SETTING
	TALE	speech to tape (unedited)	face-to-face turn taking, narration, prompting, elaborating	dream explicit: forest etc. implicit: India, Hindu dieties etc.	actual: store room tape-recorder etc. in school
G E N R E	STORY	word processed and written (edited)	not face-to-face monologue, narration without prompting, incorporating elaboration and prompts from Tale	as above plus explicit mention of some previously implicit (edited)	imaginary: content of dream beyond school (England and India)

Notes

1 See discussion of Kingman, Cox and ENC in Chapter 3.
2 The full text is given in Chapter 14 which treats the story in greater detail.
3 See *Spoken and Written Language* (1985) by M. A. K. Halliday (London: Oxford University Press), and *Orality and Literacy: The Technologizing of the World* (1982) by Walter Ong (London: Methuen).
4 This is a convenient over-simplification. Content words do express grammatical relations too, of course, and the distinction between the two types of words is not always clearcut. Function words, or 'grammatical items' form closed sets of words such as 'can', 'could', 'will', 'would', 'may', 'might', 'must'. There are just seven of these kinds of verb, whereas the number of nouns is uncountable.
5 This point is brought out in *Factual Writing: Exploring and Challenging Social Reality* (1989) by J. R. Martin (London: Oxford University Press).
6 See the publications of the National Writing Project, in particular *Audiences for Writing* (1982) (London: NFER/Nelson).

7 | *Language variation*

Types of variation

The language of texts varies in two broad ways: according to where the speaker comes from, and according to what they are doing. The former is known as dialect, and is associated with accent; the latter is known as 'register' or 'functional variation'.[1] Dialect is acquired at home. It is the way our parents speak. Functional variation is learnt as we take on social roles.

Something has already been said about a special dialect, standard English (SE), and its associated accent, received pronunciation (RP). This is special in the sense that it is based not on the geographical region the speaker comes from but the class they come from. Also, because of the prominence of this class, standard English also acts as a functional variant as well. It is used for all kinds of formal occasions, and in most written texts. For most children, standard English is learnt for use on those occasions. So *for them*, it is also a functional variant. ENC requires it as a school dialect at level 7.

General comments on accent and dialect

Strictly speaking 'accent' refers to pronunciation, while dialect refers to the words and structures used. For example, a Jamaican will pronounce the word 'hat' as 'at', 'station' as 'steshaan'. A cockney will also say 'at', 'bruvver' for 'brother', and so on. The words are the same. The way they are pronounced differs. Dialect refers to differences in the actual wording. A Jamaican will say 'me know', as against the rural Hampshire 'I knows' and the standard English 'I know'. These differences in grammar *are* just differences. None is more or less 'correct' than others.

Vocabulary differences often depend on content. When Jamaicans refer to 'rice and beans' they mean what standard English speakers refer to when they say 'rice and peas'. In Nigerian English, 'flirting' means actually being promiscuous, whereas in British standard English it does not. Someone from Leeds will say 'ginnel' where a Londoner would say 'alley'.

Dialects usually involve accents, and so the two terms overlap in meaning. Also regional dialects, that is, all dialects except standard English, are very seldom written down. This is because the British education system has always taught writing in terms of the standard dialect. The exception is where in a novel or play written in standard dialect, regional characters are introduced. When this happens adjustments are made to the spelling because the English spelling system is most closely associated with standard English and it is felt that non-standard dialects require non-standard spelling.

But differences in accent alone do not really require this. If a Birmingham child is given a page to read his or her rendering will sound different from the same page read by a Devon child, if in fact the children speak with regional dialects. The same printed marks can be pronounced in a very wide variety of ways. For example, the word 'thumb' could be expressed in the following ways:

'thum' (SE)
'thoom' (Northern dialects)
'fahm' (Cockney)
'tahm' (Jamaican)
'tom' (Yoruba)

One spelling is not closer to any one of those pronunciations than to any other, though, because most people are most familiar with the standard dictionary spelling they tend to associate it with the pronunciation associated with standard English, that is with RP.

7.1 Interaction and tone of voice

1 The children work with a tape-recorder giving as many different performances of the word 'yes' in answer to a question such as 'Have you seen my pencil?' The actual choice of question should relate to a particular text, such as a passage in a story, and to theme work being done in class.

2 If the children have not done this work before the teacher can prepare some sample intonations of 'yes' for the group to interpret, and then ask them to develop further ways of saying it, to be interpreted by other members of the group, or other groups listening to the tape.

3 The questions followed by a version of 'yes' can be numbered and scripted, and the script marked by an interpretation, which will be connected to the context. Examples of contexts might be:
    a Baljeet is annoyed with Darren for asking such a stupid question. He is holding his pencil.
    b Baljeet thinks Darren is accusing her of stealing. She is being polite because she is afraid of him.
    c Baljeet is going to keep Darren's pencil and is daring him to try and get it back, because she is pretty and he likes her.
    d Darren is Baljeet's deaf grandfather. She greatly respects him, even though he is always losing his pencil.

4 Go through the examples given in 3 and:
    a Relate them to MICS components from the point of view of the context.
    b Add further examples so that all MICS components are covered.

7.2 An accent and dialect notebook

1   The children keep a loose-leaf folder in which they have sections on the accents and dialects they hear on television soaps such as *Neighbours*, *EastEnders*, *Bread*, and *Coronation Street* and on accents of dialects of members of the class.

2   They also make lists of contrasts with improvised spellings such as:

'You'm coming' (Yaum koomeengg)   (Black Country)
'You're coming' (Yor kumming)   (SE)

3   As an extension activity, the children do tapes in which they imitate the speech of particular members of the class or soaps in:
   a   Specially composed poems or stories related to a particular area of Britain or an English speaking country.
   b   Versions of soaps in which the region is deliberately altered.

Dialects are associated with accents, but ENC makes a distinction between them when it says that although standard English dialect must be taught, the children are not asked to alter their accents. This means that a child whose local dialect would lead them to say 'twas' must now substitute standard English 'it was' but they can retain their long West Country 'a'.

But the theoretical distinction between accent and dialect is not so clearcut as ENC suggests. In practice home dialect *goes with* home accent. But the distinction is worth bearing in mind, especially as what is still referred to as 'bad English' is often dialect, that is spoken language which children have brought into their writing.

7.3 Dialect and drama

1   Using soaps
Devise a short project using the dialects to be found in TV soap operas, with the children rehearsing the accents, or adapting them to a different accent, using tapes or videos to provide pronunciation and dialect models.

2   Using children's dialects
Plan a scheme of work, where there are different dialects in the class, whereby the speakers provide tapes and coaching for other members of the class to perform a story or other text in that dialect, for recording on tape.

3   Assessment
Relate your schemes of work to specific strands across ATs in ENC. Bear in mind that accent and dialect may be studied for themselves, and also as a vehicle for developing other aspects of KAL and ENC.

Functional variation, standard English and context

Standard English is associated with certain contexts where formal polite interaction is required, and to a great extent with occupation. One context in which standard English is used, of course, is the educational one.

Often standard English implies power relations. We must use it because we are up before the head, or writing a letter of application for a job. The emphasis on standard English in ENC can be justified on the grounds that, practically speaking, if children are to succeed in social life they will need to be able to use standard English to get a good job, not to be laughed at, and so on. Against this view it may be objected that what is needed is a more enlightened attitude to dialect and accent, so that children are not forced to adopt standard English, nor penalised socially for not doing so. In other words what is needed is not so much for the individual to adapt his language as for society to alter its attitude towards dialect.

7.4 Standard English and genre

1 Standard English may be appropriate to a particular text for two kinds of reason:
    a because it makes communication possible, e.g. texts in which speakers of different dialects communicate;
    b because it is socially expected, e.g. in business letters.

2 The difference between the two is that (*b*) may be defied and/or change as social norms change, but (*a*) may not.

3 Make a list of types of written texts which, in a particular scheme of work you are doing or have in mind, would:
    a fall under category (*a*) above;
    b fall under category (*b*) above;
    c do not require SE.

Standard English, it must be emphasised, differs very little from regional dialects. What makes some speakers, such as Scots or Geordies difficult to understand by speakers of other dialects is their *accent*, and this, paradoxically, is made less important in ENC than dialect. The differences that do occur in dialect are conspicuous because they *are* different and so stand out for the speaker who would have put things differently. They have, unfortunately, been fastened upon in traditional grammar teaching and so have obtained a further prominence out of all proportion to their number. Anyone who watches American films very soon becomes familiar with minor variations such as the use of 'gotten' for 'got', 'sidewalk' for 'pavement', 'I just did' on some occasions for 'I've just done so', and so on. Conversely, children whose first dialect is not standard English, and who watch television or listen to their teachers, very soon acquire a passive standard English, that is they can understand it even if they do not speak it.

Functional variation and interaction

For most children then, standard English is used where the interaction is formal. But there are other aspects to functional variation than the use of standard English. One of these is physical and social distance.

Social distance is generally a matter of power. A private must say 'sir' to an officer; a sergeant may hurry a private but not vice-versa, and so on. Sometimes it may be the setting which creates social distance and a kind of power, giving the customer greater freedom to be rude than the shop assistant, for example, or constraining a host to beg people to stay longer when she secretly wishes them to go. These role-playing attitudes are shown in the tone of voice and the choice of words.

The text is affected, functionally, by what sort of interaction is going on. If one person is angry with another, and the other is trying to defend himself, the participants' tones of voice will be different. One will be performing acts of accusation, abuse, complaining, while the other will be issuing excuses, denials, pleadings for understanding, and so on. In an interview the interviewer will be demanding, questioning, guiding the course of the text, while the person being interviewed will be responding, informing, rejecting points, or be using evasions which look like answers, and only occasionally affecting the choice of topic. The interviewer may by sychophantic on the one hand or hectoring on the other. A barrister has to dominate the text, and must do it by asking a large proportion of his questions in such a way that the witnesses have to answer either 'yes' or 'no'.

7.5 Acting through speaking

1 Go through the examples given in Box 7.1 on p. 65 and those provided by you, and interpret the contextual interpretations in terms of speech acts, such as 'denying', 'snubbing', 'challenging' etc.

2 Describe both the answer, and what the answer suggests the question has been. For example, a 'flat denial' suggests that the question sounded to the answerer like an 'accusation'.

3 Devise classwork, extending Box 7.1 in which children are given a comic strip with the words blanked out and speech acts put in instead. So the first bubble might read simply 'Greeting'. The children have to flesh out these labels with actual wording, that is they have to provide the *form*, to implement the *function* indicated by the word 'Greeting' or 'Insult', 'Question', 'Reply', etc.

7.6 Text and power

1 The following is an extract from a conversation among Year 2 children. They are working out a story from the set of pictures given below. The teacher had told them to do this in five minutes without his presence. Then he would return.

Dan . . . bumble bee stung Grandad. The bumble bee died.
(*Laughter. Scream*)
Anil (*Singing*) I'm flying in the air.
Dan Won't be able to take these home.
Anil (*Loud mock crying*)
Judi I'm telling you. You'm being silly.

2 Point to specific places in the extract where the pictures affect what is being said.

3 Why is it difficult to understand some of the reactions and remarks? What do you have to do to make a sensible guess at interpretation?

4 How is the extract affected by power, both as a whole and in particular utterances?

(*Source: J. B. Heaton* Practice Through Picture (*London: Longman, 1971*))

Functional variation and content

Language is also adapted according to what is being talked about, the content. Specialist topics tend to have items of vocabulary which are particularly associated with them. Thus, the term 'lift-off' suggests space programmes. On the other hand some words take on different meanings according to the content. The word 'number' has different meanings according to whether it is used in texts dealing with popular music or with maths. It can also have the slang meaning of 'job' as in 'good number to be on'. This is also a matter of interaction since it implies an informal context.

Technical terms occur in class. For example, the children doing a project on gliding will know words such as 'lift', 'drag', 'yaw', and 'thrust'; those making up a pop song will know 'backing', 'lead singer', 'lyric', 'chord sequence', and so on. School studies have their own jargons, and one of the ways in which maths is learned is by gradually replacing a common-sense everyday talk of directions, corners and shapes with more restricted terms such as 'angle', 'vertex', and 'equilateral triangle'. Indeed, all academic work can be looked upon as an extension of people's repertoire of functional variants.

7.7 Specialist terms

1   The children make a miniature encyclopaedia about a particular area of interest to themselves, working in pairs on a common interest. An example might be 'Birds in our area'.

2   Specialist terms would come from ornithology, and include:
   a   the names of species of birds such as 'starling', 'rook', 'missle thrush', and 'song thrush';
   b   the names of parts of birds such as 'bill', 'plumage', and of types of feather;
   c   the names of colours and patterns of plumage and eggs, such as 'mottled', 'duck-egg blue' etc.

3   The encyclopaedia forms just a part of a wider project, of course, and is aimed at showing how precise naming leads to more precise observation, as well as developing a sense of belonging to a fraternity (of ornithologists) and being something of an expert.

4   **Assessment**
   a   Relate this work to as many strands as you can across ATs 1, 2, 3 and 4.
   b   What aspects of KAL does this work address?

Variation and genre

Dialect, accent and functional variation have been discussed within the broad conception of text outlined in Chapter 4. The terms 'functional variation' and 'genre' are similar and refer to the same combination of MICS components, but they are used in slightly different ways. When we are talking about functional variation, or 'register', we are thinking about the context. When we talk about genre we are thinking of the text. In Figure 7.1 the MICS components are described from the point of view of functional variation, that is, the columns are filled in with features of the context of situation which affect the medium.

Figure 7.1 *Functional variation (or register)*

	MEDIUM	INTERACTION	CONTENT	SETTING
C O N T E X T	remoteness or proximity of communicators whether edited	power relations, personal attitude, speech acts (e.g. demanding, reporting, evading) social roles being played/flouted	jargons, specialist terms	formality of occasion social conventions

Appropriateness and purpose

A key concept in ENC is 'appropriateness'. A number of statements of attainment require children to be able to develop their understanding of the ways in which texts are appropriate to their contexts, to the audience envisaged, to the purpose of the text, to the occasion on which it is used, and to the medium adopted.

Appropriateness is often invoked to replace the older notion of 'correctness', because different genres have different rules. The most common example given in ENC is the use of dialect and slang in literary texts. In the old days, saying 'ain't' or 'wopper' would be accounted 'wrong' in an abstract way, as 'bad English' wherever they occurred. ENC allows for the fact that under certain circumstances 'ain't' and 'wopper' would be better than standard English wording, because they are more appropriate to parts of a novel where the characters speak a dialect. It is more realistic to attempt to reproduce their dialect than transform it into standard English.

ENC also allows that such texts as personal letters make different functional demands than, say, letters applying for a job. In personal letters it is appropriate to write more closely to the way we speak, to use slang and the grammar we feel most comfortable with. However, there is a danger that ENC's emphasis on appropriateness may be used in an over-restrictive way, and as a way of reintroducing 'correct' standard English by the back door.[2] This happens where what is appropriate is presented simply as a matter of convention, saying 'This is the way things are done' without saying why. On this approach, a text is treated as a finished product whose genre is absolute and fixed, whereas in fact genres reflect human purposes. It is always illuminating to ask 'appropriate for whom?'

Let us take the example of the language typical of certain kinds of business letters, in which the receiver will read, 'Yours of the 15th inst refers' which uses business terms like 'inst' for 'this month' and 'yours' for 'your letter'. And then 'refers' is used to mean, 'is what I am referring to'. In a sense it would be true to say that this style is appropriate to business letters. But why? To see this, we have to ask about purposes.

One seems to be that it provides a ritual, which as in the ritual for meetings, allows the speaker to avoid any personal involvement. The use of 'refers' in this way, symptomatically, allows them to avoid saying 'I' or 'we'. There is an interactional point for this wording, then, that it keeps the reader at a distance, and presents the company as an impersonal edifice. On the other hand, the use of a ritual makes it neutral. No special innuendo can be read into the letter. This is how things are done, and it's the same for everyone. A third point is that it is brief and so it saves the manager's dictating time. Also, the sentence as a whole is a routine feature at the beginning of every letter, so the secretary is not going to forget to refer to the sender's original letter. Decisions on wording do not have to be made.

The specialist language, remote tone, compactness and routine nature of the sentence then, are responses to the context of situation, a matter of business letter functional variation. They are not just a set of arbitrary rules. Or are they? And may they not be challenged? The problem of teaching business letter as a genre in which this or that wording is appropriate, and some other wording not appropriate, is that *not all* business letters are like this. In recent times, in particular, firms have moved away from this wording and attempted to make their communications sound more human. So the use of the impersonal jargoned style is a matter of choice by the directors themselves, and depends no doubt on the kind of business, in particular how far business letters are sent to outsiders and how far to other businesses, and more generally the image the directors wish to project through their letters, including the style of letterhead and thickness of paper.

Genres, then, are not fixed. This can be brought out if, instead of presenting children with the model as a finished product, we ask them to go through the process of devising a letter style given a set of purposes. Conversely they can be asked to review a range of letters in different styles.

7.8 Café setting and café genres[3]

1 'Our café'
At your own level, look at the texts children would devise as part of a café project. They will stock, and run a sandwiches café in a classroom once a week, inviting other children and teachers.

2 MICS
Do MICS analyses of the following texts. How are they alike? How are they different?
    a Waiter's order pad.
    b Waiter's instructions to kitchen staff.
    c Menu.
    d Recipe.

3 Functional variation
How will the vocabulary tend to differ among the texts, even where the content is identical, e.g. about cheese and tomato sandwiches.

4 Constraints
Take any two of the texts in 2 and distinguish between the social and the material constraints shaping them.

5 Assessment
Relate this to as many strands as you can in AT 1 and AT 3.

It is usual, of course, for business letters to be written in standard English. This presents an image of a reliable, dignified company with 'educated' staff. But, children might decide, this may not necessarily be advantageous. It makes the company less 'friendly', less approachable. It would be worth at least considering what the advantages were of using the dialect of the area in which the business was set, and which the majority of customers used. But then, what real differences would result? The point would soon emerge that the differences between standard English and local dialects are very small indeed. Here we need to remember the distinction between material and social constraints on a text. Some aspects of the business letter are materially essential; others are socially conditioned.

Variation and deception

One justification for KAL is that language is a crucial constituent of everyday life. Not only does it give us the means to communicate, it also shapes who we are. We are brought up in and through it, and it shapes the individual personalities we have, and the way in which we perceive and organise our experience to ourselves, both as individuals and as members of a community, class or country. All texts, of course, present versions of reality, though they may claim to present reality as such.

A good way to introduce this function of language is by studying media texts. Political interviews make a good choice because here, very often, descriptions of events are contested. And a crucial characteristic of language is brought out, namely, its capacity to deceive. Language would not be language if it could not be used to lie.

Children enjoy deception games. These can be set up in various ways. One is to have an interview in which the person interviewed has to conceal something, and yet at the same time answer the interviewer's questions. Let us imagine the question, put to the guilty person, 'Who broke the window?' The rule is that any legalistic trick is allowed but the person interviewed must not directly lie. They may:

(*a*) respond in an over literal way to a form of words, e.g. 'a stone did', 'a boy in class 3 did' (the speaker being a boy in class 3);

(*b*) employ bluster to put the questioner on the defensive, using power, status or 'Force of character', e.g. 'Are you accusing me of being a vandal?'; 'I refuse to answer such insulting questions!'; 'Do you realise who you're talking to?';

(*c*) employ distraction, for example by going off at a tangent, by saying something like 'Do you realise your zip is undone?'

This kind of work can be connected to more specifically political interviews, for example over widely discussed issues such as the poll tax, or in relation to work on history where, let us say, Hitler is interviewed about his intentions towards Czechoslovakia and tries to mislead the interviewer. Another genre in which bias can be seen is the advertisement, or in texts which contain an element of advertising, such as a menu or poster.

7.9 Lying and partly lying

1   Devise a scheme of work in which children explore the ways in which the truth can be side-stepped without actually lying. It should be based on interviews with role play, and lead towards a video film.

2   The story board should be photocopied and the children given the task of discussing what the people are doing in and through speaking, and the tricks the interviewed person uses to evade the embarrassing questions.

3   The work can be done at a joke level, in which the evasions are absurd and over legalistic but in a manner of speaking 'logical', e.g. 'I didn't pull the cat's tail. I held it and the cat pulled.'

Conclusion

Language variation is central to the KAL component of ENC. In this chapter the discussion of language variation is, in fact, an elaboration of the model of how texts work, which was given in Chapter 4. This is because the way in which texts work is controlled by what purposes they have and what constraints there are on them, both social and physical. The variation in language, then, is simply the effects of variation in context. The most important interactive feature in the context is power. This affects, not just the ways in which politeness or domination is expressed, but textual etiquette and custom as well.

7.10 Texts, purposes and constraints

Make brief notes on the ways in which the following kinds of text are affected by aspects of the context, and by purposes. Distinguish between material and social constraints. Relate these to at least two typical linguistic details in each.
a   Headlines.
b   Sports commentary.
c   Sergeant drilling a squad.
d   Love letter.
e   Formal invitation to a wedding.
f   Computer program instructions.

Notes

1   Functional variation is the newer term for what used to be called 'register' in the earlier writing of Halliday and other systemic linguists. Halliday himself uses the term 'functional variation' in recent work. See *Spoken and Written Language* (1985) by M. A. K. Halliday (Oxford: Oxford University Press, p. 44).
2   See Chapter 3, footnote 13.
3   See Chapter 15 for a fuller treatment of this kind of work.

8 | *Early literacy*

KAL, literacy and texts

It has been stressed that KAL must be conceived on a whole-school basis. Enlightened ideas about language cannot simply be switched on at Level 5.

All early literature involves KAL because children cannot learn to read and write without knowing very basic facts about written language and written genres. They need to know what letters and words are, what stories are, what notices and labels are for, and so on. And much of this early KAL has to be made explicit to children.

8.1 Classroom writing

1 Visit an infants classroom and make a note of all the written genres to be found in it – labels, notices, diagrams, books, calendars, timetables, etc.

2 Take one example of each of five different genres and discuss the ways in which it may be used to enhance literacy. Bear in mind that the mere presence of words on the classroom walls does not guarantee that the children use them.

3 Make out a brief scheme of work by which classroom labels are woven into structured activities so that the children must read them to do the work. Concentrate on how they are to interact by means of the labels.

The teaching and learning of early literacy is a huge subject and cannot be tackled here in any detail; all that can be done is to provide a framework within which teachers can evaluate and plan their classroom practice.[1]

Reading and writing

Reading and writing should be learnt together.[2] Learning to read as a process entails recognising that reading is an active process of constructing meaning from a text, and that this text has been devised by someone with communicative purposes. Conversely, writing entails recognising that the process of writing draws upon prior knowledge of texts which have been read. In a sense, reading is a form of composition, and composition a form of writing.[3] Indeed, KAL is often addressed best by having children write for each other, or to compose scripts for performance.

8.2 Writing at the VDU screen

1 Preliminary
Children need an introduction to this work, and so at first will work in a group with the teacher, or other adult, at the computer.

2 Program operation
Children learn to start up and operate the program, reading screen instructions.

3 Story telling at the screen
Teacher, at first, acts as secretary and types a story composed collaboratively by the group. Attention is given to discussion of exact wording, and selecting alternative wording, and selected spellings, editing, format and so on.

4 Reading as reviewing
As the composition goes forward the children read at the screen in order to review what has beeen done from the point of view of editing, and what is to come next, whether the text is coherent, and so on. Spaces are left for later illustrations, and captions put in.

5 Printing and reading
The text is printed, one copy per group member. Illustrations are now done to fit the captions. This necessitates reading in order to make the illustration appropriate.

6 Reading as performance and revision
The texts are then read for a taped performance for younger children, the pictures drawn attention to. At this point revisions can be made to the script and reprints done, including extra passages by different individuals.

7 Binding
The book is now bound in as strong a way as feasible for the class library. The page sequence must be checked, and the cover title designed and made in big letters.

8 Assessment
Make a list of the ways in which this work promotes children's KAL:
- a at the level of context;
- b at the level of text.

Early literacy often features in media controversies about educational standards. All too often, here, the teaching methods are treated in the most simplistic and confused manner, in order to produce controversy. It is thus vital for teachers to have a clear professional grasp of the issues so that they can justify what they do in class and explain it convincingly to parents.

The single most important idea to grasp here is that teaching early literacy must take account of a basic fact about language, namely that it is organised in 'levels', sometimes called 'strata'. Language can be understood as a three-level system by which meaning is expressed as words and structures, and these in turn are expressed as sounds or written symbols. The three levels of a text are themselves in similar relation to the context. This is illustrated in Figure 8.1. Figure 8.1 also shows how context can narrow down the range of possible meanings a word may have. The word 'mate' has different meanings in the contexts of friendship, wildlife, chess, and seafaring.

Figure 8.1 *Levels of language and context*

C **O** **N** **e** **T** **n** **E** **c** **X** **o** **T** **d** **e** **d** SITUATION	Topic of text, people involved and their status, roles, attitudes, backgrounds, emotions, setting(s). Overall point of the communication. Determinants of medium, interaction, content, effect/relevance of setting, e.g. meeting a friend.
i **n** **T** **e** **E** **n** **X** **c** **T** **o** **d** **e** **d** DISCOURSE	Medium, interaction, content, setting. The meanings and attitudes the speaker wants to convey, e.g. greeting a friend.
a **s** **e** **n** **c** **o** **d** **e** **d** FORM	The words and grammatical structures by which discourse is carried out, e.g. 'Hello mate'.
a **s** SUBSTANCE	The speech sounds or written symbols which make the form tangible to the ear or the eye, e.g.: *Speech*: /hlou meit/ *Writing*: 'h' + 'e' + 'l' + 'l' + 'o' + space + 'm' + 'a' + 't' + 'e'.

The three levels of a text can be understood in a rule of thumb way by considering a schematised process of uttering. First we have a purpose in communicating (text) and something specific to say (discourse); then we arrange it according to the grammar and vocabulary of a particular language (form), then we make speech sounds or written marks to make it public (substance).

Early reading strategies

Reading at the level of context

The so-called 'whole books' or 'real reading' approach focuses on the levels of context and discourse. It is essential to look into the literature on this approach carefully, partly from the point of view of answering parents' questions, in part because almost all media discussions have misrepresented it.[4]

In order for children to learn to read they need to think of it as an activity, and to see adults reading in realistic situations and for credible purposes. The teacher needs to think of the MICS components of the text to be read as a product of a context and purpose.[5]

8.3 Short written texts: cards

1   Short written texts are useful for early literacy because they present a limited task, and yet can be used as realistic communication. Cards often have specific purposes such as:
   a   postcard;
   b   sorry card;
   c   invitation card;
   d   birthday card;
   e   congratulations card.

2   **Using the text**
   a   *Sending and occasion*
   Cards fit into contexts, that of going to the post office and responding to an occasion such as a wedding, being on holiday, or an exam success.
   b   *Purpose*
   First they are shown the overall use the text has, for example to show you to remember, to apologise, to commiserate, invite and so on.
   c   *Format*
   This involves drawing or pasting a picture and fitting a small number of words to it. The small number of words gives scope to concentrate on creating spellings and letter forms.

3   **Interaction**
   The children form the habit of sending cards to each other frequently for as many occasions as they can think of (congratulating someone's mum on the new baby, reminder cards to each other or teacher about outings, promises made, thank you cards for helping with work, and so on).

---

4 Planning

Sketch a session in which you get children to devise cards for a number of occasions such as the coming school holiday, apologising and mending a friendship, announcing an occasion, and so on. For each one work out how you would present the children with a task which would make them think about the design of the card from the point of view of its purposes, including being posted and having to stand on a shelf.

Children come to school with a grasp of context and the way written language is used in their lives, and hence with a good deal of knowledge about print. They can recognise the 'M' of MacDonald's, the print on cornflakes packets or the boxes of favourite toys. KAL at this stage, in the reception class, needs to be directed towards capitalising on this knowledge and developing it in kind.

8.4 Reading at the level of discourse

1 Idea

Seeing reading aloud as a ritual, concentrating on the interaction between reader and audience, and physical aspects such as turning pages, and speaking.

2 Reading as drama

The children use a book with a small amount of print, or none, and play the part of someone reading aloud, turning pages, moving eyes, and so forth. The story may be one they have heard and know, or it may be one made up previously by the reader reading from their own scribble imitations of writing.

3 Content

The words they utter have to make sense and have to make a coherent story related to the pictures, and may echo the wording of stories the performers have previously had read to them: 'Once upon a time . . .', and so on.

Books are very complex texts compared to labels, notices and bus signs. They have conventions as to the relation of the illustrations to the text, the direction in which the text has to be read, the pages turned and so on. KAL here depends on the children seeing models, joining in with the activity of story reading, and miming reading as part of their play.

Reading at the level of discourse

Writers on reading have emphasised that the texts which children read should be 'real' in the sense that they should have a point, namely to tell someone something. This is the fundamental point about reading: the exchange of meanings. Children need to understand that this is why people read. A standard criticism of the narrow approach to reading is that over-concentration on the interpretation of print leads children to think that reading consists simply in uttering appropriate verbal sounds in order to finish the page and please the teacher.

8.5 Isolating speech sounds: alliteration

1 Rap

The children take any short sentence from other work, and fit it to a rhythm produced by an electronic keyboard. For example, 'Today we learnt how to make a glider'.

2 They then edit the line:
   a   to make it easier to fit into the rhythm;
   b   to introduce alliteration (and/or other sound repetition).
   For example, 'Today we drew a design for a glider'.

3 Group composition
   a   Children work in groups.
   b   They compose one line each on the same topic.
   c   Each person in turn, says their line twice.
   d   Those not speaking are:
       i   at the keyboard (one or two people);
       ii   operating the tape-recorder;
       iii playing percussion instruments.

4 Note on keyboard

The keyboard player plays automatic chords, counting four on each of the following chords C,F,G,C. A second player can be introduced, playing notes in the treble, any notes so long as C corresponds to the final bass C chord. Keys can be marked in felt-tip.

5 Assessment

Relate this work to the idea that children's spelling (and reading) is enhanced by the ability to isolate individual speech sounds.

Thinking about what the text means helps children to predict what words and structures are likely to crop up. Prediction is the fundamental skill used by adult readers. KAL is entailed here because the skill with which someone can predict is an indication of their implicit knowledge of how texts work as wholes, what is likely to follow from what in a story and so on.

Reading at the level of form

Prediction also operates at the level of form. Children can narrow down what word is likely to come next by making use of knowledge about grammar which they already possess. Thus the end of the sentence: 'The car is in the . . .' can be predicted not only on the basis of discourse (meaning), since cars tend to be *in* garages, or perhaps tunnels, but also on the basis of form, because a noun group is required next, 'garage' or 'garage' with perhaps 'big' or 'local' before it.

Reading at the level of substance

Traditionally the teaching of reading has focused on the individual sounds of words, or 'phonics', but there is not sufficient space here to deal with this topic in any detail.[6] However, it is worth pointing out in general terms that phonics by itself, as a reading strategy, has limitations. The most striking of these is that the relationship between letters and linguistic sounds is not nearly so simple as typical phonic approaches to the teaching of reading imply. English spelling is based on a number of different systems, not just letter/sound relations. Some spellings reflect the grammar of the language, some vocabulary and etymology.[7]

Teaching children that 'c' + 'a' + 't' symbolises 'cat' is accurate in a sense, and although what we actually say when we sound it is really more like 'cuhattuh', many children learn to filter out unrequired 'uh' sounds. But all these letters also have other values, as in words like 'ice' and 'ate' and 'the'. The rules here are too complex for early readers to grasp, let alone 'apply', so they have to use other strategies anyway, strategies which they must devise themselves, and which will be based on their knowledge of grammar, discourse and context. And texts based on a limited vocabulary of 'regular' words are unlikely to sound convincing as communications.[8]

Children need to know that writing does have a phonological connection to speech. But this can be developed in ways other than misleadingly over-simplified rote 'rules'. Looking into this process is itself a form of KAL where children actually explore these connections and make their own speculations and generalisations. These will be over-simplified, of course, but adjusted to the children's own understanding, and can be modified as understanding grows. Working with rhymes, poetry or any kind of word play involving the sounds of words, is particularly valuable in recognising and isolating individual linguistic sounds.

8.6 Isolating speech sounds: rhyme

1 Rationale
Familiarity with rhymes helps children's reading and spelling, in part because the likely sounds at the ends of words differ from likely sounds at the beginnings. Rhymes, like alliterations, draw attention to sounds, and aid memory.[9]

2 Programmes of work
    a Work out a long-term policy for using rhymed poems, jingles, nursery rhymes in a particular class or year.
    b Take a particular short poem and indicate how you would begin the programme, and what sorts of tasks you would set the children to develop their knowledge of speech sounds.
    c How would you draw their attention to, and get them to discuss rhyme and speech sounds explicitly?

3 Approach to composition in rhyme
Start with the rhymes, giving the children a frame such as:

.... chat

.... sat

.... feet

.... eat

The children have to remember that words should occur in their natural sequence. They must also make sense, but metaphors can be used to 'escape' from difficulties.

A knowledge of nursery and other rhymes, and word play involving rhyme and alliteration greatly enhances this ability.[10] What is required then is 'knowledge about language sounds' of an open-ended type, based on devising, reviewing and rehearsing representations for words. Here it should be remembered that devising spellings (including marks and single letters to stand for words or ideas) contributes to reading skills.

Integrating the levels: poetry

Any serious approach to the teaching of reading needs to pay attention to reading *at all levels*. The media representation of the 'reading debate' is most seriously misleading when it implies that there is a choice between teaching at *either* substance (phonics) *or* discourse ('real' books) levels.

KAL, too, takes in all levels. Children need to know the point of the text (discourse), how it is organised (form), *and* how the print is to be interpreted as sound (substance). The thrust of the argument for working at the levels of discourse and form is that it narrows down the options at print level.

8.7 Narrowing options

1   Work with a partner interpreting the following text in which only the first sounds of words are given.
O u a t th l a gr k . H h m h , f cl , a a m c . B th k w t u .

2   What clues, besides knowledge about first sounds, did you use at the levels of:

    a   genre;
    b   discourse;
    c   form (structures and vocabulary);
    d   substance.

3   Elaborate your comments under 2 by explaining the cluster of clues which allows you to predict:

    a   the fourth word, 't ';
    b   the eighth word, 'gr ';
    c   the third word from the end, 'w '.

4   This example shows the crass over-simplification of media treatments of reading as either phonics or 'whole book'. Comment.

Reading for meaning requires that the texts have some depth and interest and so repay the scrutiny entailed to work on prediction. The condensed language of some poems is valuable here, since it motivates prediction. It holds out the interest of puzzle-solving in texts which may be extremely short. Poetry is a genre in which the reader is *supposed* to invent interpretations, and read between the lines, and often it relies on our expectation of predictable wording to create its surprises.

8.8 Reading for inference

1 Reading and expectation

All reading requires the reader to construct the meaning of the text actively from clues given in the text, some phonic, some grammatical, some to do with meaning and genre. All meaning construction requires *some* inference, and inferences depend on expectations based on KAL. In poetry, such expectations are played upon at all textual levels, forcing the reader to use greater imagination for constructing the coherence.

2 Nonsense text

This is a poem which the children are given in spoken and written form, and asked to construct interpretations for and then add further lines in the same style.

> I'm riding my breakfast to school while I'm sleeping.
> I'm drinking my tie and gobbling my shoelaces.
> I'm swimming the road. I'm steering the sky.

An example of a reading of the first line might be that the person is half asleep at breakfast thinking about riding to school, or that they are having a dream in which their breakfast is balanced on the handlebars as they ride to school.

Early writing strategies

Writing at the level of discourse

Children can compose texts before they can spell. They need first to grasp that speech can in fact be represented by marks on paper, by drawings, letters and imitation scribble writing. And they can manipulate words to make short texts before they have a detailed knowledge of their spellings or how the letters are to be formed.[11]

Work on writing at discourse level focuses on the point of writing, and so implies that the texts being written are read by other children. This reflects what has already been said on reading at this level. Here, too, is the place to emphasise the importance of presentation, the making of books for the class library, word processing, performing on cassette and video. Work at the level of discourse is work dealing with meanings, and the attempt to make meaning through writing, and to make a text as a whole hang together, and develop and gain the audience's attention.[12]

Writing at the level of form: grammar and vocabulary

There has been a long debate about the teaching of form, that is grammar and vocabulary. Most research suggests that the teaching of grammar prescriptively as correct or incorrect has little effect on the writing performance of children.[13] But this is not to say that looking *into* the ways in which words are combined in texts in an exploratory aesthetic way is without point.

For children to think usefully about form, they need to be put into situations where there is some point to this, to think about the ways in which grammar differs in different contexts, regions and genres. In particular they need to think about the difference between their own speech and the expected grammar of written genres.

It has to be recalled, also, that work on grammar needs to be connected to discourse and context, that is the text as a whole, and the genre. A wholly aesthetic approach to grammar can be sustained where children concentrate on linguistic patterning for its own sake. Here the work can also be related to maths and science.

8.9 Simple word shifting

1 Developing traditional methods

Infants commonly draw pictures of what they did during the weekend, and then dictate a caption to the teacher for them to copy. The copy element is not productive, but can be developed into a word shifting activity. For example, the child dictates 'On Saturday me and my mum went to Sainsbury's.' The teacher can split this up in keeping with the grammatical structure, the word-groups making up the clause (simple sentence), such as: 'On Saturday/me and my dad/caught/some fish'.

2 The original sentence is done on card and then cut into those strips. The child then puts them in an order, let us say, 'On Saturday/some fish/caught/me and my dad'. The teacher or other adult simply reads these back, leading the child to continue rearranging until a satisfactory version emerges. The absurd versions, of course, may be preferred as more fun.

3 Assessment
  a What is the point of this activity?
  b At what linguistic levels is KAL being developed?
  c Which ATs are addressed, or could be with adaptations?

Writing at the level of substance: spelling

Some approaches to spelling rely on children memorising whole words, which are then assessed according to whether the whole word is right or wrong. But where children are given space to explore on their own terms, they show a gradual development of spelling awareness and skill, from early attempts at spelling which simply represent words by marks, to showing whole words by single letters, then initial letters, then a selection of other relevant or feasible phonic representations.[14] This latter approach is oriented towards the children's development of spelling strategies and their discussion of the way in which spelling works. So it gives much more scope to KAL than does work oriented to rote memorising.

Writing at the level of substance: handwriting

Handwriting is the visual equivalent of speech sounds. It makes the abstract structures of a language available for others to see. From the point of view of KAL, children need to be encouraged to experiment with ways of forming letters, relating the work to pattern making, art and calligraphy, and to see the point of handwriting in communication, hence readability, and to extend this to the overall layout of the page as story, list, calculation, diagram, or whatever the text is.

8.10 Letter formation

1 Letter-making experiment
The children work in groups designing ways of making the letter 'a' (for example) in as many ways as they can, working on a large sheet of drawing paper, and using thick black felt-tip pens. They are encouraged to use aids such as circles, rulers, tracing paper, liquid paper, glue, photocopier.

2 Method
For each version, discuss with a partner, and indicate:
   a where you started forming the letter (put a red felt dot);
   b which direction the lines were drawn in (yellow arrow-head like a fish spine along the line);
   c how many different lines you had to use (a green dot at each point where you took the pen off the paper and started afresh).

3 Fluency
Test different methods of forming the letter, from the point of view of:
   a speed (measured by doing a line of, say, five and timing);
   b symmetry (measured by ruling a line along top, and bottom of the line of letters);
   c continuity (whether the letter was formed as one unbroken line).

4 Development
The work is extended to composing a concrete poem, where the design and layout of the letters in a short word has in some way to illustrate their meaning.

5 Assessment
Relate this work to *both* the cultural, and aesthetic/enabling justifications of KAL.

Hence teachers should not over-emphasise 'tidiness' as an abstraction (an expression of the teacher's power), nor put children into the position of constantly rubbing out pencil marks. A positive interest in calligraphy is enhanced by the use of sensuously satisfying felt-tip pens, colours, and good paper (where available).

Integrating levels in writing: poetry

Teaching writing requires the integration of the levels, just as does reading. This can be summed up by saying that when children are asked to write they must see that the 'lower' levels of grammar, spelling and handwriting have a communicational point, which is expressed at the levels of discourse and context. Conversely the lower levels are what allow ideas at to be communicated.

Particularly useful here is poetry, and poetic uses of language like jokes, advertisements, riddles and proverbs. Poetry is a genre in which the process by which meaning is produced is drawn attention to. The choice and sounds of words, the rhythm of the sentences, and the appearance of the text on the page are themselves a form of communication in addition to the content of the words. Also, poems can be very short, and so manageable for children to concentrate on details of language, and density of meaning. It epitomises the aesthetic approach to language study.

Later literacy

An approach to literacy in which all levels are integrated has the advantage of working with texts which are credible to children as communication. The teaching of literacy, then, does not depend on 'childish' texts. Hence the principles sketched above can be applied to the texts used by children with wider literacy, or for more mature children still developing their early literacy.

The centrality of poetry and related genres allows much more complex work in literacy to be developed in a seamless way from work in early literacy. Spelling awareness can be developed, for example, through the devising of deliberately unorthodox spellings, or expressive calligraphy and layout such as that used in concrete poetry, and the design of posters and advertisements.

Notes

1 The view of language relied on is Halliday's. The following books provide accessible explanations of it: *Language as Social Semiotic* (1978) by M. A. K. Halliday (London: Edward Arnold); *Spoken and Written Language* (1985) by M. A. K. Halliday (London: Oxford University Press); *Introducing Stylistics* (1989) by John Haynes (London: Unwin Hyman); *Introduction to Systemic Linguistics* (1975, 1977) (two volumes) by Margaret Berry (London: Batsford); *Language Education* (1989) by Frances Christie (London: Oxford University Press); *Language and Situation: Language Varieties in their Social Contexts* (1978) by Michael Gregory and Susanne Carroll (London: Routledge and Kegan Paul).

2 This is embodied in *Breakthrough to Literacy* (1970) by D. Mackay, B. Thompson and P. Schaub (Harlow: Longman/Schools Council).

3 At a theoretical level a number of post-structuralist writers have discussed this point. See *Image-Music-Text* (1977) by Roland Barthes (London: Fontana); and *Mythologies* (1983) by Roland Barthes (St Albans: Paladin). A great deal of emphasis has been placed upon the idea that there is not one final authentic reading of any text. Thus, getting children simply to play at reading by looking at print and making up words, is an important point in stressing the creative *element* in reading.

4 *Learning to Read* (1982) by Margaret Meek (London: The Bodley Head); *Language and Literacy in the Primary School* (1988) edited by Margaret Meek and Colin Mills (London: Falmer Press); *Whole Language: Theory in Use* (1985) by Judith Newman (London: Heinemann); *Reading* (1978) by Frank Smith (Cambridge: Cambridge University Press); *Read with Me* (1988) by Liz Waterland (London: Thimble Press).

5 The analysis of texts in terms of Medium, Interaction, Content and Setting combines the levels of discourse and context. The MICS components of a text can be looked at from the point of view of the text as a whole (discourse) or as forces acted on the text (context).

6 There is a vast literature on phonics. Some useful modern approaches are: 'Rhyming Connections in Learning to Read and Spell' (1990) by Lynette Bradley, in *Children's Difficulties in Reading, Spelling and Writing* edited by Peter D. Pumphrey and Colin D. Elliott (London: Falmer Press, pp. 83–100); 'Learning to Spell, Learning to Read' (1990) by Suzanne Cataldo and Nick Ellis in *Children's Difficulties in Reading, Spelling and Writing* edited by Peter D. Pumphrey and Colin D.

Elliott (London: Falmer Press, pp. 101–25); and 'Attitudes to Language and Language Teaching' (1979) by W. Harpin in *English in Education* **12**, 2.

7 See *The English Writing System: notes towards a description* (1972) by Kenneth Albrow (London: Longman); and *Language and Literacy* (1980) by Michael Stubbs (London: Routledge).

8 The coping strategies children perforce adopt to make the simple kind of phonics needs emphasising, since the standard attack on Frank Smith's 'whole language' or 'real books' approach is that it relies on coping strategies like this, whereas phonics, it is alleged, does not.

9 'Rhyming Connections in Learning to Read and Spell' (1990) by Lynette Bradley, in *Children's Difficulties in Reading, Spelling and Writing* edited by Peter D. Pumphrey and Colin D. Elliott (London: Falmer Press, pp. 83–100).

10 See note 9.

11 The method used in *Breakthrough to Literacy* (1970) by D. Mackay, B. Thompson and P. Schaub (Harlow: Longman/Schools Council) allows this.

12 See 'Learning to Write: a process of learning how to mean' (1983) by Frances Christie in *English in Australia*, **66**, (Dec), pp. 4–17; 'Writing in Schools: Generic structures as ways of meaning' (1986) by Frances Christie in *Functional Approaches to Writing* edited by B. Couture (London: Frances Pinter); *Factual Writing: Exploring and Challenging Social Reality* (1989) by J. R. Martin (London: Oxford University Press); *The Meaning Makers: Children Learning Language and Using Language to Learn* (1986) by Gordon Wells (London: Hodder and Stoughton).

13 See, for example, 'Attitudes to Language and Language Teaching' (1979) by W. Harpin, *English in Education*, **12**, 2, and 'The Difficulty of Grammar' (1947) by W. J. Macauley, *Journal of Educational Psychology*, **17**.

14 Absolutely essential reading here is *Children's Creative Spelling* (1986) by Charles Read (London: Routledge and Kegan Paul). See also the papers in *Children's Difficulties in Reading, Spelling and Writing* (1990) edited by Peter D. Pumphrey and Colin D. Elliott (London: Falmer Press); and in *Language and Learning: An Interactional Perspective* (1985) edited by Gordon Wells and John Nichols (London: Falmer Press).

Knowledge about language and the National Curriculum

Part Four is intended primarily as a reference chapter in which the different statements of attainment in ENC are interpreted in terms of the KAL entailed in them. It needs to be remembered, of course, that in actually planning programmes we begin with the idea for work. This arises from what we think as suitable practice and draws upon our general knowledge of teaching, and of language. We then look back at ENC for assessment purposes, and perhaps to check that there is a sufficient range of texts and MICS. And when we look back at ENC we look first for the overall orientation provided in the programmes of study.

It may be argued that this Part is, even so, oriented too much to the statements of attainment, and too little to the programmes of study, and that it thus encourages teachers to pay too much attention, in planning, to the latter. This criticism has its point, but on the other hand the intuitions of most teachers to check their schemes against the statements of attainment is a sound one. The programmes of study do give a more global view, but in the end it is in terms of the statements of attainment that assessment has to be done and most teachers understand that there are other factors involved here than pedagogical ones. In a sense it is they, as much as the children, whose work is being monitored by the aspect of the Education Reform Act which deals with record keeping, and due weight needs to be given to this pressure, especially as the strands in the statements of attainment are more precise than the indications of work given in programmes of study, and so, potentially call teachers the more sharply to account. Furthermore, the standard assessment tasks also are structured against statements of attainment. This point has been stressed by Myra Barrs. She writes, 'Though the rhetoric of the National Curriculum depicts PoS as the programme for the curriculum while presenting ATs as the framework for assessment only, even a brief consideration of criterion-referenced assessment shows that this kind of assessment is designed to impact on curriculum, and is implicitly linked to educational objectives. The ATs, therefore, constitute an alternative programme for the curriculum – and the only one which will be subject to assessment.'

This part, then, provides an ENC-oriented review of ideas dealt with in Part Three. The format to be followed is simply to reproduce the statements of attainment for Key Stage 1 and Key Stage 2, with the examples erased, and KAL examples put in. Nothing explicit will be said about the anomalies of ENC. These perhaps will be clear to the reader as they go through the examples.

Viewing ENC as potential for KAL means seeing how a particular strand can be satisfied in terms of text devising, text reviewing, and text rehearsal/performance. From a textual point of view there is often very little difference between statements of attainment at different levels, since essentially the same texts are required, though at different levels of sophistication. The examples showing KAL will be filled in, across the levels, from the point of view of a whole-school project on gliders, focusing predominantly, but not entirely, on the preparation of an end-of-project exhibition.

To re-emphasise, then, the aim of this exercise is to show that KAL can be found in a variety of forms in any classroom work. It is not a basis for actual planning. The key point is that KAL is to be found in almost all work, and indeed underlies the notion of good practice ENC puts forward when it lays emphasis on collaborative talk about language in activities such as drafting and editing, and attention to audience, purpose and textual conventions.

Part of the box work is assessing which statements of attainment are addressed in the work mentioned. From the point of view of the teacher's own KAL, the ability to see the range of KAL work which might be assessable under the different statements of attainment is extremely important from the point of view of planning.[1]

9 | *Speaking and listening*

Attainment target 1

The majority of KAL-texts are oral. They entail collaborative discussion about other texts, often written ones, but not necessarily. A rule of thumb for assessing KAL under a particular statement of attainment, is simply to interpret the examples given, in terms of devising, reviewing and rehearsing/presenting. This shows that KAL is as much an approach to teaching method as a sub-topic in its own right. A second approach is to assess KAL as content, for which there is indeed scope in ENC.

Examples of KAL in AT 1

LEVEL	STATEMENTS OF ATTAINMENT	EXAMPLE
1	Pupils should be able to:	
	a) participate as speakers and listeners in group activities, including imaginative play.	Collaborative devising of a glider exhibition poster. Rehearsing a taped commentary to be listened to by visitors. Planning a sequence of drawings to show how a glider was made.
	b) listen attentively, and respond, to stories and poems.	Group discussion, rehearsal and performance of a glider story or poem devised by the group for a video. Inventing rhymes, alliterations relating to poetic names of gliders.
	c) respond appropriately to simple instructions given by a teacher.	Collaborative devising of text with genre rules given by the teacher, e.g. explanation in exactly ten words, or to fit into a precise space on the poster. Collaborative sequencing of captions for photos.

9.1 Talk in school

1 Devise a scheme of work based on conversation in school, but outside the classroom: playground, secretary's office, dining-room, etc. It should take the form of a research project done by the children.

2 The aim is to get the children interested in noticing how they talk, and to do some action research of your own, perhaps using a concealed tape-recorder (e.g. in the dining-room). Points to notice (with the children) would include:

    a basis by which we recognise from the words alone where the conversation takes place;

    b effect of status and power on how children talk to each other, dinner-lady, teacher, headteacher, etc.;

    c how children cooperate when unsupervised, who dominates and how and why.

3 *After* you have done some of this work, note down all the AT 1 attainments that it covers, or could be reoriented to fulfil.

9.2 KAL and media language

The chart shows part of ENC AT 1 with the examples deleted. In the examples column enter ideas of your own which represent work on:

a KAL;
b media texts.

Specify for each example which of the MICS components is most relevant, and make sure you obtain a spread of genres (i.e. different MICS components are highlighted in different examples).

LEVEL	STATEMENTS OF ATTAINMENT	EXAMPLE
3	Pupils should be able to: a) relate real or imaginary events in a connected narrative which conveys meaning to a group of pupils, the teacher or another known adult. b) convey accurately a simple message.	

c) listen with an increased span of concentration to other children and adults, asking and responding to questions and commenting on what has been said.

d) give, and receive and follow accurately, precise instructions when pursuing a task individually or as a member of a group.

4

a) give a detailed oral account of an event, or something that has been learned in the classroom, or explain with reasons why a particular course of action has been taken.

b) ask and respond to questions in a range of situations with increased confidence.

c) take part as speakers and listeners in a group discussion or activity, expressing a personal view and commenting constructively on what is being discussed or experienced.

d) participate in a presentation.

9.3 Reading aloud

1 Working with a group of friends, take any short children's story you use or would use in class and rehearse how you would read the opening page.

2 Make amendments to the text to ensure that it is fully understandable and so that children can join in with the performance.

3 Listen to each other's performances and make suggestions to each other for improvements.

4 Assessment
a   How is KAL involved in this? Which aspects of the texts and MICS components were most prominent?
b   What terminology did you use to refer to specific aspects of someone's performance?
c   How could this work be adapted to classroom work done by the children in a particular class you teach or might teach? Outline a plan for a session on reading aloud by children working in groups. How are they to be kept on task?
d   Which strands in AT 1 apply to the work?

LEVEL	STATEMENTS OF ATTAINMENT	EXAMPLE
2	Pupils should be able to:	
	a) participate as speakers and listeners in a group engaged in a given task.	Development of L1(a).
	b) describe an event, real or imagined, to the teacher or another pupil.	Devising, discussion, and rehearsal of glider story with puppets or models for video film, or other narrative with pictures.
	c) listen attentively to stories and poems, and talk about them.	Development of L1(b).
	d) talk with the teacher, listen, and ask and answer questions.	All aspects of L2(b) above with teacher taking part and advising.
	e) respond appropriately to a range of more complex instructions given by a teacher, and give simple instructions.	Development of L1(c).

3

a) relate real or imaginary events in a connected narrative which conveys meaning to a group of pupils, the teacher or another known adult.

Development of L2(b).

b) convey accurately a simple message.

Devise a shorthand vocabulary of flight control and report words, on the model of *mayday*.

c) listen with an increased span of concentration to other children and adults, asking and responding to questions and commenting on what has been said.

Development of L1, 2(a) and 2(d).

d) give, and receive and follow accurately, precise instructions when pursuing a task individually or as a member of a group.

Development of L1 and 2(e).

9.4 One activity: many ATs

1 Draw up a plan for a morning's work in which the children prepare an aspect of an exhibition of their work, or a presentation, for other classes to see, and have explained and demonstrated. Mention the level and the topic.

2 See how many AT 1 strands you can draw into it from the point of view of KAL.

3 Make a list of the texts used and give simple MICS analyses of each.

LEVEL	STATEMENTS OF ATTAINMENT	EXAMPLE

Pupils should be able to:

4

a) give a detailed oral account of an event, or something that has been learned in the classroom, or explain with reasons why a particular course of action has been taken.

Development of L1(a), (b), (c), 2(b).
Editing written poster texts.
Meetings and debates focused on the planning of the exhibition as a whole.

b) ask and respond to questions in a range of situations with increased confidence.

Meeting, debate, reviewing and editing of witten texts and oral performances cited in L4(a).

c) take part as speakers and listeners in a group discussion or activity, expressing a personal view and commenting constructively on what is being discussed or experienced.

As in L4(b).

d) participate in a presentation.

Summation of the glider work as a whole.
Discussing textual layout and impact.

5

a) give a well organised and sustained account of an event, a personal experience or an activity.

Summation of glider work.

b) contribute to and respond constructively in discussion, including the development of ideas; advocate and justify a point of view.

Development of L4(c) and previous strands.

c) use language to convey information and ideas effectively in a straightforward situation.

Summation.

d) contribute to the planning of, and participate in, a group presentation.

Summation.

e) recognise variations in vocabulary between regional or social groups, and relate this knowledge where appropriate to personal experience.

Collaborative compilation of a glossary of gliding and aspects of aeronautics: 'flaps', 'drag', 'roll' etc.

9.5 Theme work on 'how we talk'

1 Plan a series of sessions to last about half a term in which children do KAL on 'how we talk' at KS 2 levels. The work should cover both regional and functional variation.

2 Indicate:
   a the overall aim of the work;
   b how all MICS components are catered for;
   c mention samples of texts to be collaboratively
      i devised;
      ii reviewed;
      iii rehearsed.

3 List the ATs involved, and give the specific strands for just one level with explanations where needed as to how the work fulfils them.

9.6 Disconnected narrative

1 In groups, children record one of their own stories on a tape-recorder with two spools. The teacher then dubs a second copy, and on that cuts passages of about the length of a short sentence at several points in the story. The group is organised with a narrator, character voices, tape-recorder operator, sound effects person, etc.

2 The cut version is then given to other groups to discuss and to suggest fillers for the gaps so that the text makes sense again. Note that the groups will have to be organised so that all members have contributing roles.

3 **Assessment**
   a How does KAL come into this?
   b Which strands in AT 1 are fulfilled?

9.7 Composing to a framework

1 Children listen to one or more of the following examples, and then devise their own similar short texts. Adapt or replace the examples if you think they are not suitable for the class you have in mind, or have ideas for texts which are directly connected to other work you are doing.

2 Before the session, experiment with the electronic keyboard. Put on a rhythm and practise fitting the words to it in rap style. Then make the recordings for the children.

3 Sample short texts

a In the corner of the kitchen, Kate kept a crocodile, and she called it Krikko-Krok With The Crumply Scales.

b Giant Fred
grinned and said:
'I ain't ate
vem liw kids yet.'

c I like it when it's Christmas time.
I love it when it's Christmas time.
I love it when it's Christmas day.
I love it when it's Christmas.

4 Assessment

a Relate the work to as many strands in AT 1 as you can, and give brief explanations as to how the strand is fulfilled.

b Relate the work to any two strands from AT 2 and AT 4, or make minor adaptations so that you can.

9.8 Adjusting language to audience

1 The children must think of two situations for improvised drama:

a in which great politeness is required;

b in which it would be natural to get angry.

They rehearse these in groups, organised so that they take turns to play the role of director, and interchange the parts.

2 Then they bring in unusual characters who act politely when they should be angry, angrily when they should be polite. They must, however, discuss and devise some motivation for the unusual behaviour other than 'he is mad'.

3 Begin by thinking of the situations for yourself in case the children need prompting. Pay particular attention to the role of the setting and of power relations, and where exactly the orthodox response differs from the unorthodox one.

4 Assessment

a How is KAL involved in this work?

b Which AT 1 strands are fulfilled? Explain briefly how.

10 | *Reading*

Reading and KAL

In interpreting AT 2 from the point of view of KAL we need to emphasise active forms of reading, that is discussion of reading among children, group or paired reading, and above all the interrelationship between the development of reading and writing, which the format of ENC tends to undermine. And we need to emphasise the process of reading, which involves not just the reader and the text, but the writer, and the writer's awareness of the reader.

Reading as such can be done alone, but KAL is usually best promoted in the context of rehearsal and performance for an audience. And if the 'script' here has been composed by the reader/performer the interdependence of reading and writing is underlined.

Reading can be analysed in terms of the typical KAL processes of devising and reviewing, but AT 2 cannot be viewed in isolation, since almost all KAL requires two texts, one of which will usually be oral (AT 1) – that is the KAL-text. When we look at reading we are looking at an interface between the text being read (the content text) which is written, and the act of reading and talking through the reading (which is oral). Thus, in an actual classroom reading session, aspects of AT 1 and AT 2 will be open to assessment simultaneously.

10.1 Meshing ATs

1 Look through *any three* statements of attainment (strands) for AT 2 for either L1–3 or L3–5. For each of the strands make a note of any kind of talking and/or listening which the work might entail.

Example
AT 2 L2(a): 'read accurately and understand straightforward signs, labels and notices.'
This also involves speech and listening:
    a If the signs, labels and notices are devised by a group for a practical classroom purpose.
    b If the signs, labels and notices are used in a practical activity such as for:
        i directing a toy car along a route;
        ii card games such as 'snap' using words;
        iii badges;
        iv classroom resources such as 'string', 'elastic bands', 'glue'.

2 Assessment
In what ways is KAL entailed in this box?

10.2 Reading as writing: writing as reading

1 Take any piece of writing or a transcribed recording done by one of the children. Make a typed or printed version and sufficient photocopies for a group.

2 How will you organise a session in which children use the text for group reading so that they feel the reading:
- **a** has an interactional and communicational point *as writing*;
- **b** involves doing something active;
- **c** leads to a tangible outcome.

3 Points to consider:
- **a** How can children discuss *interpretations* of the text?
- **b** Should you make alterations yourself to make the text:
  - **i** more accessible?
  - **ii** less accessible?
  - **iii** more orthodox in spelling or grammar?
  - **iv** contain more repetition?

4 Make a note of the AT 2 strands which this work would fulfil.

10.3 Print carries meaning

1 Collecting short texts

The children collect short texts from the school or home setting. Examples would be the lollipop lady's 'STOP', 'Macdonalds', street names, notices such as 'Toilets', cornflakes and other packets, cartons and wrappers. These would be photographed, or cut out to preserve the original lettering.

2 Sorting

The collection is kept in a group loose-leaf folder or pocket file. The groups are given work sorting the texts in different ways, for example, according to:
- **a** the setting in which the text is usually found;
- **b** what sort of interaction it involves, e.g. persuading, warning, informing, commanding;
- **c** what content is associated with it, e.g. cornflakes, the school bus, hamburgers.

3 Assessment
- **a** Note all strands in AT 2 level which could be fulfilled (at different levels) by the sorting work.
- **b** Which KAL themes does it address?

10.4 Drawing as a record of experience

1 Infants visit a zoo or historical site, or simply go for a walk around the school field. They 'make notes' of what they have seen by drawing small quick sketches as aids to memory. This is done on a small pad.

2 They exchange and compare notes in groups and work out how they could sequence and paste-up a combined and revised version, which would be understood by other groups.

3 They pass this to another group who read it, and come back to them with queries about unclear symbols.

4 A class wide-picture glossary of all symbols used is displayed on the classroom wall.

5 **Assessment**
   a What aspects of KAL does this work address?
   b Which AT 2 strands are entailed?
   c How can the work be taken forward and related directly to:
      i spelling?
      ii composition?
      iii reading?
   d How would aspects of the history of writing systems be related to this work?

KAL in AT 2

In the examples of KAL given, it is assumed that the children will be working collaboratively on tasks, and hence talking explicitly about what they are doing. Hence the success of the work depends crucially on the teacher's ability to ensure that the children actually go through the processes mentioned.

LEVEL	STATEMENTS OF ATTAINMENT	EXAMPLE
1	Pupils should be able to: a) recognise that print is used to carry meaning, in books and in other forms in the everyday world.	Devising labels at the concept keyboard and using them on • glider diagrams; • for boxes/drawers or modelling materials. Devising drawings and using them as aids to memory 'writing'.

b) Begin to recognise individual words or letters in familiar contexts.

Printing out and using initials and key words for:
- name on wings of own glider;
- posters/diagrams with 'flaps', 'wings', 'fuselage' etc.;
- for use in concept keyboard composition;
- instructions on table-tennis-like 'bats' for test flying, such as 'Michael go'.

c) show signs of a developing interest in reading.

Summative of other strands in L1.

d) talk in simple terms about the content of stories, or information in non-fiction books.

Reading drafts of each other's picture sequence and caption texts about:
- experiences of imaginary/model glider pilot;
- diagrams/posters explaining glider making, gliding process.

Making suggestions for improvements, display, and preparing tape for exhibition visitors to listen to with earphones.

Play reading glider stories and glider picture sequences, provided by teacher or children.

10.5 KAL and group reading

1 Reading a story

Take any good children's story and plan how you would organise a session of group reading for infants in Y1. The aim of the work is to make children use a range of reading strategies, to be conscious of these, and at the same time to be relatively independent of supervision.

2 Orientation to strategy

Look back at the discussion of reading and language levels in Chapter 8. The children's strategies should be based on using the following kinds of clue:

  a the picture (discourse: setting);
  b what event is likely to occur next and why (discourse: content);
  c what word or words are likely to come next (form);
  d what the characters might be thinking or planning (discourse: interaction in the story);
  e what the children have absorbed of phonics (substance: medium);
  f how the story is likely to end (discourse: genre).

3 Drama

Think of the work as, in part, drama. The children must *play the parts* of readers and listeners. If they get stuck they must *invent* something plausible, which is subject to discussion with others, and to other suggestions.

4 Management

Consider the following practical matters:
   a preventing one child from dominating the talk;
   b preventing interruptions and quarrels about turn-taking;
   c making sure all children have a role;
   d making sure the children understand the task.

5 Assessment

   a Make a list of ATs and strands involved.
   b How would this work be adapted to Y5 juniors who have a command of basic reading?

10.6 KAL and the alphabet

1 Devise *five* activities which require children to use the alphabet.

2 Think of texts in which the alphabetic sequencing, and/or the use of initials of different kinds would actually be used.

3 Outline an activity showing the text in realistic use, for example:

Lettering on the wings of a model glider. The letters are to indicate:
   a the name of the owner and the 'mark' of the glider this one represents;
   b the class and group they belong to and the place of the glider in the alphabetical order of the test flight schedule.

Thus,   *Left wing*   *Right wing*
          JH – B   C4D – J

Which means:
'John Haynes'   'Mark B'   'Class 4 Group D'   'Flight order J'

4 Assessment

   a What kinds of KAL are entailed in each activity?
   b Do a MICS analysis for two of the examples.
   c Identify two strands at any one level in AT 1, AT 2, AT 3, AT 4, and AT 5, which could be addressed in one or more of the texts you have outlined.

LEVEL	STATEMENTS OF ATTAINMENT	EXAMPLE
2	Pupils should be able to: a) read accurately and understand straightforward signs, labels and notices.	Development of L1(a). Devising tags for glider's wings based on glider name, maker's initials, class, group, etc.
	b) demonstrate knowledge of the alphabet in using word books and simple dictionaries.	Using initials of child's own name and friends. Development of L1(b). 'Alphabetical order' for • test flying in groups; • classroom storage of models; • captioning pictures/photos.
	c) use picture and context cues, words recognised on sight and phonic cues in reading.	Development of L1(a). Development of mime reading. Allocating preprinted captions to glider photographs, pictures.
	d) describe what has happened in a story and predict what may happen next.	Completion of lines in a 'glider rap' (see Box 9.7). Begin glider stories for other groups to complete.
	e) listen and respond to stories, poems and other material read aloud, expressing opinions informed by what has been read.	Tapes for exhibition stalls, describing and elaborating: • friends' glider stories; • diagrams, models, pictures. Conversational narratives about glider topic experiences.[1]
	f) read a range of material with some independence, fluency, accuracy and understanding.	Summative.

10.7 Talking about narrative

1   At your own level, working with a friend, take any story or film you both know, and make a diagram of the narrative as it is a sequence of events.

2   Try to fit this into the following general scheme:

Stable state of affairs.
Complication which threatens or upsets normal state of affairs.
Attempts are made to remove the complication.

The complication is resolved.
Stable state of affairs.
(*Further complications may be introduced at any point.*)

Throughout the story there is also, generally, some way in which what is happening is evaluated as good, bad, terrible, frightening, evil, exciting, and so forth.

3   What application does this knowledge about narrative have in the classroom in relation to reading? Which strands in AT 2 does it address?

4   How would you use this scheme in getting children to:
   a   talk about *Jack and the Beanstalk*?
   b   develop a story of their own for group reading or performance?

5   Here is a possible opening for a children's story. It stops at the point where the complication is about to be brought in:

'I had a pet baby alligator. It was called Rotagilla. Dad fixed up the garden shed for it. And he put an old bath in there for Rotagilla to swim around. And he had a heater put in too. Every day, after I'd had my breakfast, I took Rotagilla his food. And then I walked to school. But, one morning . . .'

6   Suppose you presented this to your class and asked them to continue the story. *You* try to guess what aspects of the stable situation they:
   a   would most likely use;
   b   could possibly use to make a complication.

7   Work out a teaching plan whereby you took the story forward bit by bit with groups, and fulfilled strands in AT 1, AT 2 and AT 3 in roughly equal proportions.

10.8 The content of factual texts

1   Selecting facts
Working in a group at your own level, look at a particular small room. Then, individually, without consultation make a list of what you see. Restrict yourself to twenty items.

2   Categorising facts
Still, individually, arrange the list into three sets and represent the sets in a diagram, i.e. of 'types of thing'.

3   Discussion
Now look at each other's work. Consider:
   a   why some items but not others are excluded or included;
   b   what set of priorities each member of the group had for categorisation.
Take another person's categorisation and rearrange his/her items on the basis of a different set of categories.

4   Classroom

Briefly outline the ways in which this kind of activity could be used by children in a class you teach or might teach.

5   Assessment
   a   How does this work constitute KAL:
      i   from the point of view of cultural knowledge?
      ii from the aesthetic (or enabling) point of view?
   b   Which strands in AT 2 can it be used to fulfil?

10.9 Signs and actions

1   Control

Devise a classroom activity in which written signs are used to control what children do. This might be:
   a   traffic control with toys;
   b   PE activity;
   c   musical score for percussion.

2   Aims

The aims of the work from the point of view of KAL are to show that signs:
   a   imply practical responses;
   b   must be brief enough to fit onto a small area;
   c   must be unambiguous.

3   Assessment

Do a MICS analysis of one sign you envisage and show:
   a   how it is related to any of the KAL themes mentioned in Part Three;
   b   which AT 2 strands it fulfils in KS 1.

LEVEL	STATEMENTS OF ATTAINMENT	EXAMPLE
3	Pupils should be able to: a) read aloud from familiar stories and poems fluently and with appropriate expression.	Script and story board for a video, reviewing items in the exhibition. Development of L2(e).

c) listen attentively to stories, talk about setting, story-line and characters and recall significant details.

Development of L2(e), L3(a).

d) demonstrate, in talking about stories and poems, that they are beginning to use inference, deduction and previous reading experience to find and appreciate meanings beyond the literal.

Making and interpreting riddles and proverbs.
'Lateral thinking' about short passages, haikus, nonsense texts, codes.

e) bring to their writing and discussion about stories some understanding of the way stories are structured.

Development of L2(d).
Composing to a given framework.
Devising stories around a given 'exciting moment'.
Development of L2(d).

f) devise a clear set of questions that will enable them to select and use appropriate information sources and reference books from the class and school library.

Development of L2(b).
Writing a gliding encyclopaedia.
Contents pages for stories and other texts.

4

a) read aloud expressively, fluently and with increased confidence from a range of familiar literature.

Development of L3(a).

b) demonstrate, in talking about a range of stories and poems which they have read, an ability to explore preferences.

Assess and edit as a group the story boards, and rehearse voices over/character parts for exhibition video featuring:
- glider stories and raps;
- processes of model making;
- dramatisation of model pilot's experiences/adventures.

Development of L3(a).

c) demonstrate, in talking about stories, poems, non-fiction and other texts, that they are developing their abilities to use inference, deduction and previous reading experience.

Development of L3(d).

d) find books or magazines in the class or school library by using the classification system, catalogue or database and use appropriate methods of finding information, when pursuing a line of inquiry.

Development of L3(f).

5

a) demonstrate, in talking and writing about a range of stories and poems which they have read, an ability to explain preferences.

Development of L4(b).

b) demonstrate, in talking or writing about fiction, poetry, non-fiction and other texts that they are developing their own views and can support them by reference to some details in the text.

Development of L3(d), (e), L4(b).

c) show in discussion that they can recognise whether subject matter in non-literary and media texts is presented as fact or opinion.

'Is it true?' discussions of glider stories, focusing on elements of scientific fact in fictional stories. Devising video interviews with model/puppet glider pilot about flight plan, direction, experiences.

d) select reference books and other information materials and use organisational devices to find answers to their own questions and those of others.

Devising critiques of exhibition diagrams and models with:
- bias against (devil's advocate);
- bias in favour (advertisement).

Devising/interpreting secret codes or messages for glider espionage.

e) show through discussion an awareness of a writer's choice of particular words and phrases and the effect on the reader.

Development of L3(d), L4(c). Devising specialist glossary on gliding/aeronautical terminology. Rewriting instructions or explanations for younger children at the exhibition.

10.10 Using initial sounds

1 Phonics and real communication

Devise and plan the classroom organisation of work in which children use the sounds at the beginnings of words for real, or realistic, communication.

2 Real use of initials

Here are some examples of initial sounds used as such in ordinary life, which children could use as models for their own inventions:

   a   initials of people's names;

   b   common abbreviations such as BBC, TV, USA;

   c   special abbreviations such as 'u' for 'you';

   d   'secret' codes such as SWALK;

   e   acronyms such as NATE;

   f   alliterations in poems or advertisements.

3 Assessment

   a   Show how the work constitutes KAL.

   b   Relate the activity at AT 2 strands in KS 2.

10.11 Reading strategies (Year 2–3)

1 The children compose words for a song or rap. It must:

   a   repeat each line three times;

   b   fit to an electronic keyboard beat.

2 Working in groups:

   a   make a written version which the group needs to be able to understand, but not necessarily the teacher;

   b   make a taped performance.

3 Photocopied lyrics and tape are given to different groups for them to:

   a   listen and enjoy;

   b   mark the words on which the beats fall;

   c   on lines 2–4 of each set of repetitions, delete one important word per line, using liquid paper.

4 The lyrics are returned to the writers for the deleted spaces to be filled by *different* words from those in the first line of each.

5 Assessment

Comment on:

   a   the ATs and some of the strands entailed;

   b   what the children learn about the genre;

   c   what reading strategies they learn about, and how you would make this knowledge explicit.

10.12 Early reading strategies

1 Read a well-produced book to a group of reception children, allowing them to join in with suggestions, repeat passages, and to volunteer comments/ additions to the text, as well as evaluations. Tape the session.

2 Pause from time to time to discuss:
   a what is going to happen next, and how it will end;
   b how the author is going to bring in this or that particular idea or entity later in the story;
   c how a particular character ought to say something;
   d what actual words will/might come next.

3 Play back the tape, and allow similar interventions from the children while the tape is on.

4 **Assessment**
What does this sort of session teach the children:
   a about story texts?
   b about the activity of reading?
   c about reading strategies?

10.13 Proverbs

1 Any statement with a verb which indicates what normally happens can be read as a proverb. The statement is interpreted as advice as to what the listener ought to do. For example:

Statement of habitual	*Moral*
A bird builds its nest in a tree.	Don't take unnecessary risks.
The rain falls from the sky.	Be logical.

2 Give the children some practice with everyday statements you have devised, and then ask them to do the same in groups. They then pass their proverbs on to other groups for suggestd moral.

4 'Morals' done by mentioning a specific setting in which the proverb would apply, rather than as the kind of abstraction given in 1, are quite acceptable. But the point needs to be raised that different solvers have cited different possible settings. How many are there?

10.14 KAL and intonation

1 Performance

Working with a friend and a tape-recorder, prepare as many different renderings of the following line from *The Glass Menagerie*, by Tennessee Williams: 'Time is the longest distance between two places'.

2 Begin by discussing the line and then attempting to render stage directions such as philosophically, desperately, mockingly, bitterly, and so on.

3 Listen to your taped versions of these and try to formulate what it is about the way your voice rises and falls, which words are most emphasised, that changes. Do not go to books on intonation. The point is:

    a   to try to make explicit what you know and can do by intuition;

    b   to think what sorts of terms the children might need to devise when they do the activity.

4 Assessment

    a   How is this work related to the idea that reading should be for meaning?

    b   How would you devise work for children along these lines, and design it to develop reading strategies?

    c   Which strands in AT 1 and 2 are addressed in this work?

10.15 Standard English and genre

1 Spoken conversation

Sham   I buyed a mote control car and it had wires. And he had a Michael Jackson record.

Ram   And I had a Michael Jackson record. And I had a car set. It was us to share. I'm going to have a car. A big one.

Sham   And I had some books. Colouring books, and writing books.

Ram   We went to the park, and we saw some ducks and we went on the swings. And then we had some crisps. Salt and vinegar.

Sham   We changed our birthday to Saturday cause we have to go to the funeral.

JH   Where was the funeral?

Sham   I don't know. I think it was in West Bromwich.

Ram   They burnt him.

Sham   They burnt him. And sometimes they put people on water . . .

2 Rewriting as standard English

Make a standard English version of this text as a first person narrative by the teacher, and without using reported speech.

3 Photocopy the conversation given above and use highlighter pens to indicate:

    a   material you retained as it is in the conversation;

    b   material you deleted;

c   material you altered from the point of view of standard English story genre. Break this down into categories according to the types of inappropriateness you detected.

4   Write brief explanations for your decisions in **a, b** and **c** above.

5   **Assessment**
a   Which KAL themes does this exercise address?
b   How could this work at your level on this conversation be adapted to the primary classroom?

Note

1   The kind of oral story making in which the narrator is helped and prompted by the small audience. See Chapter 14 for an example of this kind of work.

11 | *Writing*

Writing, reading and talking

Writing here will be understood as 'composition', not as spelling or handwriting. Children can compose printed stories before they have acquired fluent handwriting and spelling.[1] But still, as in Chapter 10, reading and writing will be seen in a complementary way.[2] As has already been mentioned, KAL almost always entails oral work, the collaborative discussion of what to do next. So all the examples mentioned in this chapter will also address comparable strands in AT 1 and AT 2.

KAL in AT3

LEVEL	STATEMENTS OF ATTAINMENT	EXAMPLE
1	Pupils should be able to: a) use pictures, symbols or isolated letters, words or phrases to communicate meaning.	Devise symbols, initials, logos to: • put on wings of gliders; • instruct test playground flyers through the window from inside the classroom. Devise small-scale sketches as aids to memory for: • what we did on gliders today; • how to set the flaps.

11.1 Concept keyboard writing composition

1 Idea

The work is designed to allow children to compose without needing to handwrite or spell. It links composition with reading, and with recognising the connection between print and language, and requires 'chronological' sequencing.

2 Children are given a set of four (or more) pieces of paper of about postcard size. They draw a series of pictures which tell a story. The story should be:
  a connected to other work to be done;
  b fact, fiction or faction;
  c done in black biro and felt-tip (for photocopying).

3 They put the pictures into sequence and help each other to tape-record their stories. Where possible, they integrate pictures from all the group.

4 Photocopy the pictures and reduce them in size so that they can be pasted onto a concept keyboard overlay. Pressing a picture on the concept keyboard overlay produces a short written phrase on the screen. Avoid 'linking' words such as 'so', 'then', 'and', etc.

5 The children develop as many different stories/sequences as they can, filling in the link words between them orally when they read.

6 **Assessment**
  a What KAL is involved here?
  b Which ATs and strands are involved?
  c How would you develop this text for use at the top of the junior school, bringing out the idea that pictures and writing are not related in a straightforward way?

11.2 Connecting words

1 Develop Box 11.1 so that the children have to focus on, and use, connective words such as 'so', 'then', 'and', and so on.

2 Do this with different kinds of texts (genres), and consider yourself which connecting words are most likely in which genres.

3 **Assessment**
Relate the work, as developed, to all relevant strands in AT 3.

11.3 Exciting moments

1 Present the children with examples of 'exciting moments', such as:

'And then it smashed down the whole building.'
' "Don't force me to do that!" the little goblin screamed in tears.'

2 The children must discuss what has happened immediately before, what the setting is, what is about to happen, and who else is involved, and later, how the situation is to be resolved.

3 First, they use exciting moments provided by teachers to devise stories orally; then they try to devise their own exciting moments and, as a group, shape a 'before' and 'after' and 'who else' story around these.

4 A development would be for a number of exciting moments to be sequenced to make a more complex story.

5 Assessment
  a What features of story structure does this work focus on?
  b Which ATs are addressed?

11.4 Speech and writing

1 Conversational story telling
In a group, the children tell a story and tape it. There is one storyteller and three listeners who prompt, ask for clarification, and contribute ideas. The story must be no more than *three* minutes long.

2 Transcription and editing
The teacher transcribes the tape with all the ums and ers in it, and the children then edit the transcript so that there is just one narrator, and turn it into a written story.

3 Questions about editing
Consider the following problems, bearing in mind the level at which the children are working:
  a What aspects of the tape *must* be altered?
  b Should punctuation go into the teacher's transcription?

4 Assessment
  a Review the ways in which this work bears on the KAL theme dealing with the differences between speech and writing (see Chapter 6).
  b Relate the work to as many strands across the ATs as you can at one level.

LEVEL	STATEMENTS OF ATTAINMENT	EXAMPLE
2	Pupils should be able to: a) produce, independently, pieces of writing using complete sentences, some of them demarcated with capital letters and full stops or question marks.	Devise captions for gliding exhibition poster, photos, diagrams etc. Devise gliding and glider raps with pauses.

b) structure sequences of real or imagined events coherently in chronological accounts.

Devise picture stories and put in captions and speech bubbles, for:
- what we did on gliders today;
- adventures of model glider pilot.

c) write stories showing an understanding of the rudiments of story structure by establishing an opening, characters, and one or more events.

Taping group conversational anecdotes about work done on gliding, or personal experience of or about it, and:
- editing transcriptions to make written stories;
- making written versions without using transcription.

Inventing 'exciting moments' for a model pilot's adventures.

d) produce simple, coherent non-chronological writing.

Development of L1(a) and L2(a).

3

a) produce, independently, pieces of writing using complete sentences, mainly demarcated with capital letters and full stops or question marks.

Development of L2(a).

b) shape chronological writing, beginning to use a wider range of sentence connectives than 'and' and 'then'.

Development of L2. Also linking mixed-up sentences and phrases using specified words such as 'and', 'so', 'but', 'and yet', etc.

c) write more complex stories with detail beyond simple events and with a defined ending.

Development of L2(c) on 'exciting moments', using 'unexpected ends'.

d) produce a range of types of non-chronological writing.

Development of L2(b).

e) begin to revise and redraft in discussion with the teacher, other adults, or other children in the class, paying attention to meaning and clarity as well as checking for matters such as correct and consistent use of tenses and pronouns.

Devising and preparation of public versions of exhibition posters, published forms of stories, etc.

11.5 Lines, pauses and punctuation

1 Idea

The aim is not to go directly to punctuation as a 'right or wrong' phenomenon. The work deals with those aspects of a text in which punctuation is connected to speech rhythm.

2 Task

The children work in a group to perform the following kind of text arranged in lines. A pause is to come at the end of the line. Stress falls on the emphasised words.

> We made a *glider*
> with *wood*
> and *glue*
> and a rubber *band*
> to keep on the *wings*

3 They then experiment by changing the lengths of the lines, and discuss how this changes the performance, and where line ends can and cannot come.

4 They then compose their own texts indicating pauses and stresses in the same way; and pass them to other groups for performance.

5 Assessment

Place this work in a wider perspective, linking it to the teaching of punctuation proper, and how this link could be effected.

11.6 Grammar as verse

1 Making nonsense

The teacher takes any text and alters the content words into nonsense words. Here is an adaptation of the opening of *The Owl and the Pussy Cat*. Note that endings such as 'ed' and 'ful' are retained.

> The Kwip and the Doppy Dut relled to slib
> in a trockaful groy doit mib.

2 Preparation

The children work first with texts they know and reconstruct them from the nonsense versions and make nonsense versions of their own to exchange with other children.

3 Development A

Then they make, or make use of, their own rap texts, such as:

> I'm riding my bike to school in the morning
> [*I'm plimbing my swoot to liep in the toal*]
> My bike's very smooth and quiet
> [*My swoot's very sleer and wod*]

I'm speeding smoothly and quietly to school
[*I'm kreating sleely and wodely to liep*]

4   Development B

They make nonsense versions into which particular 'rules' of spelling, or grammar are built. For example:

  a   nonsense words must all have two syllables;
  b   nonsense words must not sound English;
  c   two nonsense words per line must contain an 'ea' spelling;
  d   both function and content words must be substituted for other English content and function words.

5   Assessment

Which strands in both AT 2 and AT 3 does this work address?

LEVEL	STATEMENTS OF ATTAINMENT	EXAMPLE
4	Pupils should be able to:	
	a) produce, independently, pieces of writing showing evidence of a developing ability to structure what is written in ways that make the meaning clear to the reader; demonstrate in their writing generally accurate use of sentence punctuation.	Development of L3(a).
	b) write stories which have an opening, a setting, characters, a series of events and a resolution and which engage the interest of the reader; produce other kinds of chronologically organised writing.	Development of L3(c). Adapting glider poster for younger children, non-specialists.
	c) organise non-chronological writing for different purposes in orderly ways.	Drawing a diagram as plan for explanation of how flaps affect a glider's flight.

d) begin to use the structures of written standard English and begin to use some sentence structures different from those of speech.

Rearranging word groups in different grammatical patterns:
● as aesthetic/poetic game;
● to decide which is clearest.
Redrafting transcriptions of oral discussions of test flight for written versions, as:
● report;
● minutes of meeting.

c) discuss the organisation of their own writing; revise and redraft the writing as appropriate, independently, in the light of that discussion.

Development of L3(e).

11.7 Grammar as pattern

1 Aim

Getting children interested in grammar as imaginative pattern making and problem solving.

2 Word groups

The teacher cuts up a clause into word groups and puts them on cards. If you find the following method over-complex use your own or cut the clause up at random. The cards correspond to word groups, and each type of word group is given a different colour:

This orang-utang	was	riding	my bike	megadudishly	to school
Blue	*Red*	*Green*	*Blue*	*Brown*	*Yellow*

3 Working with one clause (simple sentence)

The children arrange the cards to make as many different clauses with the example as they can. They can use all or some of the strips, and the results need not be 'complete sentences'. They make a copy of each structure, and must be able to explain the meaning of each example they make in terms of either:
   a context;
   b co-text (that is, what has come just before in the text).

4 Reviewing grammar and meaning

They classify their results.
   a Versions more likely in speech or in writing.
   b Versions requiring completion of some kind.
   c Sequences of colour which cannot occur sensibly.

5 Development

a Groups devise abstract patterns of the strips, such as 'Blue Blue Red', work out wordings, and get other groups to interpret them.

b The same pattern is repeated to form several lines for another group to fit in any new words they can which conform. This builds up a poem in a grammatical metre.

6 Assessment

How can this work be justified in terms of AT 3 and KAL?

11.8 Engaging interest

1 Preparing a story for younger children

The story must be connected to other theme work, and must be performed both on tape or video, or live, and printed with illustrations.

2 Research

The children visit the class concerned, looking at their work, topics, and interviewing them about stories most enjoyed and about interests. They also interview the class teacher.

3 Devising/drafting/editing

They prepare a text using ideas gathered from research, and try a draft out on representatives from the target class, asking for responses and criticisms. They revise the story in the light of criticisms. Some audience participation should be planned.

4 Rehearsing/editing

They prepare a performed tape with announcer, narrator, actors, music, sound effects, using dubber to cut and alter. Repetitions should be increased here.

5 Book

They make a book/script from the tape and get it typed or printed, and design where illustrations are to go (separate squares pasted in).

6 Performance

They perform the story and advertise the book of it for the younger children to read afterwards.

7 Assessment

Relate the work to KAL themes and AT 3 strands.

11.9 Quotations

1 Planning a comic strip

The children plan a comic strip in small groups. They should include two kinds of writing:

    a commentative captions referring to the picture in an oblique way without reproducing in words what the picture shows;

    b speech bubbles for what the characters actually say.

2 Changing the genre

They reshape the comic strip as a story without pictures to help:

    a on tape with changes of voice;

    b as fiction using quotation marks for previously bubbled words.

3 Development: speech acts

Fiction involves language about language when it comes to dialogue words like 'said', 'replied', 'stammered', 'flashed' etc. These words often describe 'speech acts', that is, what people are doing in and through speaking. Get the children to:

    a Blank out the actual words in the speech bubbles of a comic strip and insert, instead, the speech act being performed, for example 'asking', 'commanding', 'refusing'. The speech act version of the strip is then passed to a partner to suggest actual wording.

    b The teacher puts wording into blanked out speech bubbles. But the wording does not obviously follow a coherent thread. The children have to use inference to make sense of the bubbles, by working out what the speakers are thinking to make them respond to previous speech bubbles, as they do. After some experience of this children can do the blanking out and rewording themselves.

Example

First speaker's bubble: Hello, Michael
Second speaker's bubble: The dragon!

4 Assessment

Link this work to as many strands in AT 3 as you can, making brief notes as to what aspect of the work relates to which strand.

LEVEL	STATEMENTS OF ATTAINMENT	EXAMPLE
5	Pupils should be able to:	
	a) write in a variety of forms for a range of purposes and audiences, in ways which attempt to engage the interest of the reader.	Development of L4(b).

b) produce, independently, pieces of writing in which the meaning is made clear to the reader and in which organisational devices and sentence punctuation, including commas and the setting out of direct speech, are generally accurately used.

Development of L4(a).

c) demonstrate increased effectiveness in the use of standard English (except in contexts where non-standard forms are needed for literary purposes) and show an increased differentiation between speech and writing.

Development of L4(d). Devising dialogue, speech bubbles for fictional glider pilot, and contrasted with his entries in his log after test flights.

d) assemble ideas on paper or on a VDU, individually or in discussion with others, and show evidence of an ability to produce a draft from them and then to revise and redraft as necessary.

Development of L4(e).

e) show in discussion the ability to recognise variations in vocabulary according to purpose, topic and audience and whether language is spoken or written, and use them appropriately in their writing.

Devise stories with pilot jargon and diagram using aeronautical terms, either orthodox or devised by group.

Notes

1 This is the important insight embodied in *Breakthrough to Literacy* (1970) by D. Mackay, R. Thompson and B. Schaub (Harlow: Longman for Schools Council).
2 The interdependence of reading writing is shown in 'Some Notes on Learning to Read' in *The Language of Primary School Children* (1973) by Connie and Harold Rosen (Harmondsworth: Penguin Books). In their chapter of 40 pages on reading they devote 24 pages to writing.

12 | *Spelling, handwriting and presentation*

As previously, the work cited in the KAL example column is assumed to be collaborative and broadly discussion-based with the emphasis on the processes of devising and reviewing texts in the context of topic work on gliding.

KAL in AT 4 and AT 5

LEVEL	STATEMENTS OF ATTAINMENT	EXAMPLE
	Pupils should be able to:	
1	a) begin to show an understanding of the difference between drawing and writing, and between numbers and letters.	Making captions for glider photographs, drawings, using own improvised or scribbled writing.
	b) write some letter shapes in response to speech sounds and letter names.	Development of L1(a). Initialling code for identifying: • glider's owner, e.g. G-PH (Glider-Paul Hughes). • parts of the glider, e.g. l.w. or p.w. for left wing or port wing on diagrams and plans.
	c) use at least single letters or groups of letters to represent whole words or parts of words.	Development of L1(b).

12.1 Spelling and pictures

1   The children have a set of small pictures on cards, and a set of function words on slightly smaller cards. The content words are taken from topic work they are already doing. The function words are words such as 'the', 'this', 'he', 'is', 'she', 'and', varying in variety and number according to the children's experience, and those which the children recognise.

2   Working in pairs within small groups, they invent statements by arranging the pictures in sequences linked by the function words. Then they pass them to another pair in the group for interpretation.

3   **Assessment**
   a   Formulate to yourself how this work can enhance the children's spelling skills.
   b   Which strands in AT 4 does the work address?
   c   What other aspects of language, beside spelling, does the work impinge upon?

12.2 Different systems of spelling in English

1   **Pattern completing**
Complete the following patterns, and discuss with a friend, what the basis of the spelling pattern is. Note that they are not all based on 'phonics'.
   a   sign, signature, . . .
   b   bits/bids, laps/labs, . . .
   c   judge, George . . .
   d   slow/cow, tow/how, . . .
   e   to/two, so/sow, . . .
   f   give, live . . .
   g   Jorj, ej, . . .

2   **Application**
What teaching strategies would you use to develop children's knowledge of spelling patterns other than those based on phonics?

3   **Assessment**
Relate this work to relevant strands in AT 4.

LEVEL	STATEMENTS OF ATTAINMENT	EXAMPLE
2	Pupils should be able to:	
	a) produce recognisable (though not necessarily always correct) spelling of a range of common words.	Produce glider and gliding texts using a mixture of pictures or drawings, initial letters followed by dashes, and function words, e.g. My /picture of glider or 'gl——'/ is r (red).
	b) spell correctly, in the course of their own writing, simple monosyllable words they use regularly which observe common patterns.	Interpret, and later make, initial letter 'riddle' texts on a known topic, introducing common function words and content words (in whole or part) prominent in the glider work, e.g: T—— we fl— our gl——s. (*Today we flew our gliders*)
	c) recognise that spelling has patterns, and begin to apply their knowledge of those patterns in their attempts to spell a wider range of words.	Making oral and then written glider poems and raps to simple metres such as: • four beats per line; • two alliterations per line; • two occurrences of '–ing' or 'in–'; • rhymes or near-rhymes such as 'Fly'/'high'; or 'fly'/'glide'.
	d) Show knowledge of the names and order of the letters of the alphabet.	Using alphabetical numbering and initial labelling in classroom and topic management, e.g. for storing model gliders along the shelf in alphabetical order.

12.3 Spelling and talking

1 Idea

Children's spelling and reading are enhanced by the ability to isolate speech sounds. Poetry is particularly useful for this. It allows children to concentrate on particular sounds while at the same time developing their sense of the genre.

2 Poetry and speech sounds

Below are some methods of directing attention to speech sounds by giving children a metre to work to. They might include:

a Stress: so many beats per line. Begin by using rap and fitting stressed words to the beats.

b Syllabic: so many syllables per line.

c Grammatical: fitting into a framework or two lines or more, such as:

'My xxxxxx is xxxxxing to the xxxxxxx'

I xxxxxxx s/he xxxxxxs some xxxxxxxx'.

d Fitting words into a frame which gives the first sounds of words, such as:

'T . . . . w . . . . . * . . . . . * . . . . . . p . . . . .

(* = free choice of first sound).

e Alliterative: so many alliterations per line.

f Fitting words into lines for which rhyme sounds or rhyming words are given, e.g.

. . . . (s)ound

. . . . (p)ound

g A combination of these.

3 Assessment

Make notes on ways in which this activity fulfils, or could be developed to fulfil AT 4 L1(c), L2(b), L3(a) and L4(a).

12.4 Initial texts

1 The children are given a short account of work done previously. The account is written, by the teacher, wholly in initials, using clusters such as 'pr', and digraphs such as 'ch' and 'th'. They are told the content and setting. An example would run:

Y	w	d	s	w	o	gl
(*Yesterday*	*we*	*did*	*some*	*work*	*on*	*gliders*)

2 They have to solve the puzzle, counting any sensible or humorously absurd readings as successful. They then invent their own initials texts in groups and pass them around.

3 Development

Instead of limiting the initials to whole words, we can compose texts in which the initials of *syllables* are given, thus drawing attention to polysyllables, and noticing the initial letters of these. Thus, the polysyllables in the example would become

Y st d   gl d

4 Assessment

a Note AT 4 strands that are addressed.

b How could this be used also in AT 2?

c What implicit KAL does a child need, apart from a knowledge of initial sounds, to interpret the initials text?

LEVEL	STATEMENTS OF ATTAINMENT	EXAMPLE
	Pupils should be able to:	
3	a) spell correctly, in the course of their own writing, simple polysyllabic words they use regularly which observe common patterns.	Development of L2(b). Development of L2(c). Also making the rap beat coincide with syllables to produce frames such as 'Gl—d—' (glider) 'st—b—' (starboard).
	b) recognise and use correctly regular patterns for vowel sounds and common letter strings.	Poems, and poetic names using rhyme and vowel alliteration, e.g. 'slide glide', 'higher flyer', 'air ace'. Maths-oriented word sorting in sets defined by aspects of spelling. Art-oriented pattern making and concrete poems for exhibition posters, book covers, etc.
	c) show a growing awareness of word families and their relationships.	Development of last two items in L3(b), e.g. maths/art patterns based on: 'glide/glider/gliding/ glides/glided'; 'fly/flight/flyer'; 'high/height/higher'.
	d) in revising and redrafting their writing, begin to check the accuracy of their spelling.	Summative: aspect of reviewing texts for exhibition.
4	a) spell correctly, in the course of their own writing, words which display other main patterns in English spelling.	Summative.

12.5 Spelling sets

Idea

Spelling is only partly phonic. Some thinkers say it is best learnt from a wholly visual approach. Here we reflect on some words which have already been read and are familiar in work on a story, *Little Red Riding Hood*. The point the work is aimed at bringing out, is that English spelling is based on a number of differing but overlapping systems, some phonic, others not.

Sets

Here is a sample of the words laid out in sets. Children have to devise an explanation based on the spelling as to why the words are set as they are, a common spelling factor for each set. *Any* explanation is valid; it does not necessarily have to be the rule an adult would pick out. The point is to get the children to look into and discuss how language is represented in writing.

Set A: (grandmother, growl, great)
Set B: (see, me, tea)
Set C: (girl, wolf, shelf, beard)
Set D: (loved, felt, spilled)
Set E: (love, live, gave)
Set F: (bee, be)

Development

The children devise a card game based on the vocabulary used. This should be one in which the winner of the trick is able to provide a convincing reason why a hand, or other group, of cards has one spelling factor in common. A more sophisticated version might be to give different spelling factors different values so that, for example a set of words related by having the first letter 'c' would carry less value than one which was related through all being words ending in latinate suffixes.

12.6 Skeletons and patterns of spelling

1   Words can be indicated just by using the consonants. Thus:

'Ystrd w dd sm wrk n gldrs'

Reading this has the effect of drawing attention to the vowels, by their absence. And in general the consonants are more predictable at the level of phonics than are the vowels.

2   When the children are asked to try to fill out these skeletons they have first to think where vowels might fit. Even the wrong vowel in the right place represents an important insight into how English words are structured.

3   **Assessment**
    a   How can skeleton writing be developed further so that typical spelling patterns emerge for the children?
    b   How can this sort of work be made into a communicative activity? Or a game?

KAL in AT 5

LEVEL	STATEMENTS OF ATTAINMENT	EXAMPLE
	Pupils should be able to:	
1	a) begin to form letters with some control over the size, shape and orientation of letters or lines of writing.	Calligraphy for the letter initial designs on glider's wings, and for aspects of class organisation.
2	a) produce legible upper and lower case letters in one style and use them consistently (i.e. not randomly mixed within words).	Making initial texts (as in AT 4 L1(a), L2(a),(b)), one-word labels, gliding logos.
	b) produce letters that are recognisably formed and properly oriented and that have clear ascenders and descenders where necessary.	Making patterns based on common shapes in words used in L1, L2(a).
3	a) begin to produce clear and legible joined-up writing.	Development of L2.
4	a) produce more fluent joined-up writing in independent work.	Summative.

12.7 Word families

1 In *TV Centre*, Frame 1, (see Figure 4.1, p. 37) Bruno's bubbles could have been:

a 'And Craig McLachlan enters with a new number at nineteen.'
[*Word family resemblance: 'entry', 'enters'*]

b 'And Craig McLachlan's new number makes an entrance in the nineteenth spot.'
['*entry*', '*enters*', '*entrance*']['*nineteen, nineteenth*']

2 Thus upper junior work could link children's grasp of word relations to work on editing and rewriting. Variation like that illustrated above is required in genres like DJ presentation because they are potentially very repetitive. And monotony is just what the DJ must avoid. So here stylistic variation and indeed exhibitionist language, are appropriate.

3 Devise some realistic settings, and how work would be organised, where children need to make stylistic variations of this kind, bringing out word families. Examples might include song lyrics or poems with repeated lines with small variations each time.

12.8 Playing the system

1 Children with some familiarity with the spelling systems of English can become more explicitly aware by devising unorthodox versions which flout the rule normally followed, but follow another present elsewhere in English. This can be assimilated to aspects of poetry, and perhaps 'concrete' poetry. For example:

'flight' → 'phlight' → 'phlite'
'are' → 'ar', 'ah', 'R'
'Let her see' → 'Letter C'

2 Activities

a Invent a text on the basis of 'minimum number of letters per word'. (well → wel, etc.).

b Do a rebus language text (drawing of an eye = 'I', with C = 'see', fx = 'effects'). This can be developed to near equivalences such as Z = 'said'.

c Devise a backslang based on inserting an extra syllable, for example, 'rag' after each vowel in a word and the vowel repeated after it. Thus: 'cat' → 'ca*rag*at', 'glider' → 'gli*rag*ider'.

KAL in AT 4/5

LEVEL	STATEMENTS OF ATTAINMENT	EXAMPLE

Pupils should be able to:

5

a) spell correctly, in the course of their own writing, words of greater complexity.

Summative.

b) check final drafts of writing for misspelling and other errors of presentation.

Development of AT 4, L3(d).

c) produce clear and legible handwriting in printed and cursive styles.

Summative.

Notes

1 *Words Not Numbers: Assessment in English* (1990) by Myra Barrs (Exeter, NATE) p. 15.

PART FIVE

Some programmes of work

Part Five is devoted to a description of three programmes of study carried out by the author. Two are oriented towards the development of text-making skills through KAL, the third towards KAL as ideas and facts about language.

The work described was devised independently of ENC. This fits Cox's recommendation for teachers to begin with an idea for work based on good practice, and only to look back at ENC after the main lines of work have been decided upon, as a way of assessing planning. Then, certainly, ENC may itself suggest refinements or elaborations to the project which can be incorporated into it. Checking against the programmes of study and ATs is a way of gaining further ideas, and can increase the variety of texts envisaged. This approach is not peculiar to KAL, of course.

It would be possible to work back from ENC strands, by selecting a number of these and aligning them to the same topic. The drawback in doing this is that it is all too likely to lead to a mere token adherence to the topic, and produce a succession of discrete classes which are related to, say, gliding, only very tenuously. (This likelihood is increased where the topic is based on an abstraction such as 'ourselves', or 'change', into which almost any piece of work can be assimilated.)

Chapters 15 and 16 constitute no more than sketches of what was done, and leave the reader with the task of thinking through the details of the basic idea for themselves. So the main import of these chapters lies in the boxes, that is in the reader's own reflections, criticisms and plans for work. The general method of planning KAL already discussed is shown diagrammatically overleaf.

Planning KAL

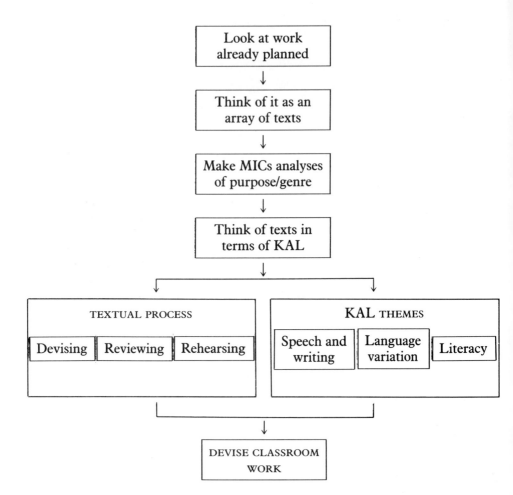

13 | *Story making*

Idea

The programme began with an idea for getting children to gain confidence and skill in composing narratives. They were all speakers of English as a second language, of Sikh background, and all under-achieving in day-to-day classwork, having problems in particular with literacy. But they were fluent orally, and Mandeep, in particular, was a good story teller. The idea was first thought of when one of the children told a story about a dream during the course of a conversation which was being taped. It was then decided to transcribe part of the taped conversation containing the story, and to present it to the children for editing to produce a written literary story. For convenience, the oral conversational story will be referred to as the 'tale', and the written version the 'story' (see Figure 13.1).

Figure 13.1   *Written texts used*

Description	Label
Transcription of the taped conversational narrative.	TALE
Word-processed sheets in which crossings out and editings/notes were entered.	DRAFT
Written story resulting.	STORY

Although most of the actual writing would take the form of transcriptions done by the teacher, the children would have to read through their transcribed tale and then do some editing to produce the story. The editing would involve making handwritten alterations to a word-processed printout. This afforded the opportunity for a manageable amount of writing which the children could concentrate upon closely, but which they could still see as part of quite a long ambitious text of their own.

KAL focus: genre

The work focused on the way in which story telling and story writing are done, and how medium, audience and purpose affect the process. The work was thus related to two broad KAL themes:

1   The way in which the tale or story maker's purposes and audience affect the text produced. This is primarily a matter of *functional variation*.
2   The difference between an oral tale and a written story. This is primarily a matter of *medium*.[1]

13.1 Tale as a genre

1   MICS

Make a MICS analysis of specific texts to show the genre of:
   a   a folk or fairy tale;
   b   an anecdote about what happened on the way to work, told later that day in the pub or at a friend's house.

2   What are the main differences between the two?

3   What would you teach children about one or other genre, and how would you go about it?

Description of the work

The group doing this work was made up of three children and the teacher. The children were related. Mandeep was Harjit's older sister, and Sona their cousin. An informal conversation was tape-recorded. During the course of the conversation Mandeep and Sona produced the tale given on pages 140–2.

Mandeep had to retain her audience by making sure that the tale was interesting and also by making sure that it was coherent. The first KAL aim was to focus on these skills, and to show how a face-to-face audience could help keep it going, that a narrative text is interactive, and that an essential element in making the text coherent is remembering that an audience have to follow it.

While she told the tale other members of the group intervened from time to time in two main ways:

1   To prompt Mandeep by making encouraging sounds, laughter, exclamations, and requests for clarification where the narration was not clear.
2   To make entries in the tale by volunteering further ideas. Most of these dealt with the mythology and were oriented towards the teacher, as the cultural outsider.[2]

13.2 Audience as co-composers

1   Photocopy the tale (see pages 140–2).

2   Look at all the turns ('speeches') by people other than Mandeep. Label each of these:
   a   prompt;
   b   entry;
   c   other (as necessary).

3 Discuss with a small group of colleagues or friends how you would distinguish prompts from entries.

4 Make a table to show how the different types of audience intervention are distributed among the members of the group, and if there is any tendency for particular members to intervene in particular ways. Suggest reasons for this.

5 Summarise the ways in which the interventions:
   a threaten the narrative;
   b enhance the tale as a whole;
   c are taken up by Mandeep later. Think, in particular about the themes of transformation and belonging.

Mandeep maintained her role well at the outset, but the number of interventions volunteering ideas increased as she went on, and the audience threatened to take over the textual initiative and turn the tale genre into a kind of lecture directed at the teacher about Sikh/Hindu deities. The teacher finally had to insist that Mandeep completed the tale, which she did, and unobtrusively incorporated ideas which had been thrown up in the interventions by Harjit and Sona, or which perhaps, Harjit and Sona were merely bringing out for the teacher's sake.

The taped tale was listened to and then the teacher transcribed it from the tape onto a Folio word-processing disk. At first it had been intended for the children to edit the work on the screen, but this proved a problem mainly because they had had no previous experience of word-processing and had difficulty scrolling the text back and forth. As a result, they were given copies of the printed version and asked to do crossings out and corrections on it.

Since they had not done it before, the children needed help with the editing. At first they were asked to think how to turn it into a tale by one person, so they had to remove all the names at the head of each conversational turn. Then they had to look to see what else had to be changed for the text to make sense.

13.3 Changing the medium

At your own level edit the tale so that it reads as a monologue. Make the minimum alterations you can. Make brief notes as to:
a interpretative decisions you have had to make when not sure how the original hangs together (coherence); and
b cuts and additions you found necessary.

We also had a number of discussions about what, to the teacher, were obscure points, despite the explanations already included about 'our God'. And the children were asked to consider which of these interventions should be embodied in the tale. In the event, they deleted a good deal of the background information. The work rests at this point, but since then the teacher has discussed the tale again with Mandeep, but unfortunately not on tape.

13.4 From speech to print

1 Make a summary of the differences between the tale and the story (see pages 140–2). Pay particular attention to:
  a what is cut and what is added;
  b how the writing differs from the speech in wording;
  c any aspects of spoken language the story retains.

2 In what ways is the story more coherent than the tale, and what remains puzzling to you?

3 Discuss the following propositions:
  a In fact the presence of the teacher is distorting. The children understand the implicit meanings perfectly well, and the tale is coherent to them.
  b The coherence of the tale simply follows the kind of coherence found in dreams.
  c The story still sounds like children's speech written down.

4 **Assessment**
  a Make a list of as many strands as you can across ATs at levels 2 and 3, which could be addressed through the work described on *Mandeep's Dream*.
  b List strands in AT 1 at any one level which could be related to KAL texts devoted to:
    i devising a content-text;
    ii reviewing a content-text;
    iii rehearsing and simultaneously devising an oral text.

A note on narrative

The role of the narrator has often been studied by scholars from the point of view of the textual coherence of the tale looked at as a completed whole. The approach taken here, however, looks at the way the interactions shape the narrative.[3]

Essentially, a narrator must provide information which is interesting and exciting, but in doing this he must make sure that he does put his audience fully in the picture. Notoriously young children, and bad tale-tellers generally, fall down here. They mention 'this' and 'it', and 'there' without identifying what is actually being referred to. It is there in their heads, but not in the audience's. The tale-teller has to tread between the two extremes of telling the audience too little, and hence becoming obscure, and telling them too much, and hence becoming boring.

In a conversational narrative the audience acts as a check on the tale-teller because they can intervene with requests for clarification or, if the tale is getting tedious, indicate their boredom by body language, or by subverting the tale in some way. They may do this politely by changing the subject, or rudely by telling the tale-teller they don't want any more.

In a written story the writer does not have this check, and so he has to anticipate what an envisaged audience would ask if present, and then build the information into the tale. He has, in other words, to pre-empt possible confusion or boredom by putting himself into the position of his imagined audience.

The children were familiar with conversational narration since tale-telling forms a prominent part of conversations of all kinds, both their own and those they will have joined into or heard among adults. This KAL can be used as a starting point. The adjustments needed for narrative with a single narrator can thus been seen to flow from the extra constraints and needs of an absent audience of readers.[4]

13.5 Beginning conversational narration

1 Model

Begin by telling a personal tale from your earliest childhood about an event which was important to you, and still often comes to mind: an accident, a loss, something very frightening, etc. Allow interventions from the class about the children's own similar experiences.

2 Children's tales

Ask the children to tell their own tales. If there are enough tape-recorders, have one per group and allocate roles such as tape-recorder operator, director, sound effects person, narrator, etc., which are rotated. You will need microphones!

3 Speech to writing

Some can be transcribed by the teacher, but the class activity will be to:

a play back the tale and talk about it;

b discuss how to merge all the contributions into one narrator's written (or taped) story;

c draft a written version together or, with younger children, prepare a sequence of comic strip type-pictures with captions and bubbles in their own spellings, or dictated to the teacher.

d discuss the draft writing/drawings and edit for a final version.

4 Assessment

a Children work in groups of three to prepare final versions to be word-processed, printed and bound for the class library.

b Devise a way in which, to develop this work, you would use this or some other, or children's, analysis of narrative structure to make the children more explicitly aware of the genre.

Attainment targets

The work falls into Key Stage 1 and involves all ATs 1–3. Taking into account the development of the individual children, the optimum levels were L2 and L3, though some of the work would impinge on L4 too.

AT 1 L2(a) Participating in a given group task.

L2(b) Describing an imagined event to teacher and pupils.

L2(c) Listening to stories and talking about them.

L2(d) Talking with teacher.

L2(e) Responding to more complex teacher instructions and giving instructions (i.e. when editing within the group).

L3(a)   Development of L2(a).
L3(c)   Development of L2(c).
L3(d)   Development of L2(e).

AT 2   L2(d)   Describing what has happened in a tale and predicting what may happen next (i.e. response and suggestions from audience to Mandeep's telling).

L2(e)   Listening and responding to a tale read aloud (i.e. on tape); expressing opinions about it.

L2(f)   Reading a range of material (i.e. reading the transcription in order to edit, forms one feature of this).

L3(c)   Listening to stories and talking about story-line and characters.

L3(e)   Bringing to their writing and discussion about stories some understanding of the way stories are structured.

AT 3   L2(b)   Structuring imagined events coherently and chronologically.

L2(c)   Writing and showing understanding of basic tale structure.

L3(b)   Development of L2(b).

L3(c)   Writing more complex stories with defined endings.

L3(e)   Redrafting in discussion with other children and adults with attention to meaning and clarity.

Narrative texts

Tale (Mandeep's dream: spoken)

1	*Mandeep*	I was in the bed, and this – I had a dream about a fox, to coming near me and had green eyes flashing to me.
2	*J.H.*	Hmm!
3	*Mandeep*	And then I was frightened. I hold my sister's hand, so we can find the place where we can . . . And we saw this old man. Had this thing and looking everywhere (*gesture*).
4	*J.H.*	A camera?
5	*Mandeep*	Yeah. And a lady said, 'Ah, these are little children. You want to come with me?' And we found a place. She told us where's the place and we found it – forest. Was all this food in. Bananas, orange, and that. And some things to eat.
6	*Sona*	Chapati. Chapati. And Roti.
7	*Mandeep*	And then we, and then we found the place. We ran. So . . . And we locked we locked the door, and then we saw this big castle down by the hill, this big castle. And there was a horse. And these doors opened.
8	*J.H.*	Yeah?
9	*Mandeep*	And the horse can get right in. And the castle was bi bigger – than all this house.
10	*Harjit*	Bigger than this school.
11	*Mandeep*	And I saw er I saw this man talking through the sky.
12	*Harjit*	You know what?

13	*Mandeep*	And he was . . .
14	*Harjit*	I saw God's leg. In the sky.
15	*J.H.*	Did you?
16	*Harjit*	All black. It was bigger than this school.
17	*J.H.*	You did!
18	*Sona*	Sir, you know our God, it's really . . .
19	*Harjeet*	You know God? He can turn into anything.
20	*Sona*	Sir? Sir, you know our God? He can change into anything. He can change into anything. He can change into you, sir. He can change . . .
21	*J.H.*	Into me!!
22	*Sona*	Yeah. He can even change into me, sir. He can change into anybody, and he's got lots of power in his er in his eyes, and all his <u>body sir.</u>*
23	*Harjit*	<u>You know how much legs he's got?</u>
24	*J.H.*	How many?
25	*Harjit*	Two hundred.
26	*Sona*	No he hasn't! He's just <u>lying!</u>
27	*Harjit*	<u>He has!</u>
28	*Harjit &* *Sona*	[*Indecipherable altercation*]
29	*J.H.*	Okay, let Mandeep go on now. That was very nice. Go on, Mandeep. You saw this voice in the – you heard this voice in the sky. Go on.
30	*Mandeep*	And then I saw the man was talking to me. And he came with – he was following with me, sir. He was just going like that [*gesture*]. [*Laughter*]
31	*J.H.*	As if he's swimming, eh?
32	*Mandeep*	He was in the sky.
33	*Sona*	What you on about?
34	*Mandeep*	Following me. And told me where my – England is.
35	*J.H.*	Oh, yes.
36	*Mandeep*	And he hold me, and my sister . . .
37	*J.H.*	Yeah?
38	*Mandeep*	With two hands. And he took . . .
39	*J.H.*	In the sky?
40	*Mandeep*	Yeah. And he took came down and took me. HERE. And then I went back to my place. I saw all these nice little birds. When he took me I nearly was falling down. And he caught me. And we went. And we saw this big lady and she had – she was in the castle doing her make-up things. And I told the man, 'Look at that lady in the castle. She's pretty isn't she?' And he said, 'Yes, she is pretty. This England is really pretty.' And she changed into a butterfly, with bright colours, sir, red and black and yellow, and other colours.
41	*Sona*	Not black! I hate black.

* Underlining indicates speakers speaking at the same time.

42	*Harjit*	God hates black.
43	*J.H.*	Why do you say that?
44	*Sona*	Sir, because black's not our real colour, sir.
45	*J.H.*	I see. What do you mean, 'real colour'?
46	*J.H.*	<u>The most important one?</u> . . .
47	*Harjit*	<u>Because, because</u> . . .
48	*J.H.*	Why? Why, Harjit? – <u>Do you know?</u>
49	*Harjit*	<u>I don't know.</u>

Story (*Mandeep's dream: written*)

I was in the bed and I had a dream about a fox was coming near me, and it had green eyes flashing to me. And then I was frightened and held my sister's hand so we can find a place where we can stay. And we saw this old man holding this telescope and looking everywhere.

And a black lady (Kalima) said, 'Ah, these are little children. You want to come with me?' And we followed her. We went in this cave. It was really big and dark. She left us there. We shouted and screamed but there wasn't any sign of anybody. Then we went outside, and fell in a hole, and the hole leaded to this forest. It had lots of fruit it, bananas, orange and pears.

Then we ran and ran. Then we saw a castle. We saw the door open itself. It was misty and dark.

And I saw this man talking through the sky. And he was . . . then I saw the man was talking to me. And he came and was following me flying. He was just going like that. He was in the sky following me. And told me where my England was. He held me, and my sister with two hands.

And he came down and took me and then I went back to my place. I saw all these nice little birds. When he took me I nearly was falling down. And he caught me. And we went. And we saw this big lady and she had – she was in the castle doing her make-up set things. And I told the man, 'Look at that lady in the castle. She's pretty isn't she?' 'Yes, she is pretty. This England is really pretty.' And she had wings like that.

And she changed into a butterfly with bright colours, red and black and yellow and other colours. 'Not black! I hate black!' God hates black. Our God said he hates black to me. It went dark. 'Cause that's not our real colour. Red's our real colour,' he said to me. 'Red is our real colour.' And he went away.

Draft[5]

MANDEEP'S DREAM

I was in the bed and I had a
dream about a fox was coming
near me. And it had green
eyes flashing to me. And
then I was frightening and
held my sister's hand so we
can find a place where we
can stay. And we saw this old
man had this thing and looking
everywhere.

~~MR HAYNES~~ *GHALIMA*
~~A camera?~~

~~MANDEEP~~
~~Yeah.~~ No

And a lady said, ^black ^lady
        Ah, these are little
children. You want to come
with me?' ^We went in this
And we ~~found~~ a place. ^followed her cave . It was really big
^a dark
She told us where's the place ^She left us there. We shouted a screamed but
^there, wasn't any
~~and we found this forest.~~ ^sign of anybody. Then we
^went outside, and fell in a
~~Was all this food~~ in. Bananas, ^hole a the hole leaded
organge, and some things to
eat ~~Ade~~. Then we found
the place. We ran. And we
locked the door, and then saw
this big ~~castle~~ down by the
hills. And there was a horse.
And the door opened and the
horse can get right in. And
the castle was bigger.
We ran and ran then we saw.
a castle. - We saw the door opened. It
~~was~~ ^as Matase the We Went in it was
^neaber ^an dack

~~HARRIT~~
Bigger than this school.

MANDEEP
And I saw this man talking
through the sky. *and he was.*

HARJIT
You know what?

MANDEEP
And he was.

God leg in the sky.

It was all black. It was bigger
than this school.

Sir, you know our God. It's
really....

HARJIT
He can turn into anything.

SONA
2 | Sir? Do you know our God?
He can change into anything.

He can change into you, sir.

MR HAYNES
2 | Into me!

SONA
Yeah. He can even change
2 | into me. He can change into
anybody. He's lots of power
in his eyes, and his body, sir.

MR HAYNES
2 | Let Mandeep go on now. You
saw this voice in the sky.

MANDEEP
And then I saw the man was
talking me me. And he came
and was following me. He
was just going like that.

MR HAYNES
He was swimming, eh?

~~MANDEEP~~

He was in the sky. And told me where
England was. He held me, and my
sister, with two hands.

~~MR HAYNES~~

In the sky?

~~MANDEEP~~

~~And he came down and took~~
~~me and then I went back to~~

And he came down and took
me and then I went back to
my place. I saw all these
nice little birds. When he
took me I nearly was falling
down. And he caught me.
And we went. And we saw
this big lady and she had -
she was in the castle doing
her makeup set things. And I
told the man,
  'Look at that lady in the
castle. She's pretty isn't
she?'
'Yes, she is pretty. This
England is really pretty.
  And she had wings like that.
  And she changed into a
butterfly with bright colours,
red and black and yellow
and other colours.
Not black! I hate black
~~SONA~~ God hates black
Not black! I hate black.

~~HARJIT~~

God hates black.

~~SONA~~

~~Sir, our God hates black.~~

~~MR HAYNES~~

~~Why do you say that?~~

~~SONA~~

~~Sir,~~ cause that's not our real
colour. Red's our real
colour. he said to me red was our real
colour and he went a 'woe

Discussions

The teacher discussed the tale with the children during the editing, and noted some of their comments on the copy of the draft reproduced. After the story had been completed the teacher discussed a number of outstanding points with Mandeep, but this conversation was unfortunately not recorded. Before this the teacher had consulted Sikh colleagues about the figures the children identified as Kalima and Lal Mata.

It emerged that the 'place' in the tale referred to India, and that the flying man was Guru Gorbind Singh who transported the children from England (symbolised by the castle) back to India and then returned her to England again. The black woman is 'Kalima' a slightly sinister female deity traditionally dressed in black.[6] The 'lady' who helps and turns into a butterfly is 'Lal Mata', another deity who is especially associated with women, marriage, and the protection of girls. She is also associated with the inner strength people have when they clear their mind of spiritual fear and have a total trust and commitment to the good.

The deeper meaning of the tale seemed to be Mandeep's search for a sense of belonging in 'this England', 'my England'. The tale still remains enigmatic to the cultural outsider, but in an enriching, and indeed intriguing way.

13.6 Wider questions

1 Coherence
Discuss in general how far you think a text like *Mandeep's Dream*, which is in its way literary, needs to be fully explicit as to its themes and progression? Do you see any danger in insisting on *explicit* coherence?

2 Creativity
It has been argued by J. R. Martin (1989) that children's creativity is different from that of adult professional writers. The latter have a secure knowledge of genre and their departures from the norms are calculated. But children, on the other hand, are struggling towards the norms of the genre and their 'creativity' is primarily a matter of adult perceptions from adult expectations about genre, creative reading by us, rather than creative composition by them.

    a   How far is Martin right about professional writers?

    b   In what ways *is* Mandeep like a 'real' writer?

Notes

1   There is a more detailed discussion of these points in relation to extracts from the spoken and written versions of the story, *Mandeep's Dream* in Chapter 6.

2   The term 'mythology' is used rather than 'theology' because the children's knowledge of Hindu and Sikh cosmology was extremely impressionistic.

3   The work also illustrates the theory of text generation developed by M. A. K. Halliday and Ruqaiya Hasan in *Language, Context, and Text: Aspects of Language in a Social-Semiotic Perspective* (1985) (Oxford: Oxford University Press). See in particular Ruqaiya Hasan's discussion of text and context on p. 55. But the approach taken in looking at *Mandeep's Dream* differs from most investigations of the coherence of children's writing in the focus it puts on the developing of

coherence through actual or tacit interaction with the audience. The work also fits into the theory as to how literary texts evolve historically from conversation developed in *Towards and Speech Act Theory of Literary Discourse* (1977) by Mary Louise Pratt (Bloomington: Indiana University Press).

4   This over-simplifies in the sense that, as the written story has evolved, it has taken on other typically writerly characteristics which do not simply flow from the immediate constraints of writing. See the discussion in Chapter 6 about the difference between material and social constraints on genre, and also the brief comments on informational density and grammatical metaphor typical of adult writing.

5   The working draft differs slightly from the text. This is simply because the text incorporates a later revision, and supplies features missed when the first transcription was done.

6   Misspelt 'Ghalima' by me in the draft.

14 | *Our café*

The idea

The children in a top junior class (Years 5 and 6) were asked to work out ways and means of running a school café selling sandwiches and soft drinks once a week in a spare classroom. They had to work out how it would be financed, stocked, the food prepared and served, classroom adapted, publicity arranged, and so on. Three teachers were involved, the class teacher and two support teachers.

Children from other classes would be asked to visit the café and so they too had an opportunity to deal with such texts as menus, oral orders for food, notices, bills and so forth. The children doing the project were organised in groups concentrating on:

1 Arranging the room.
2 Selecting and buying bread, cheese, butter etc.
3 Publicity and notices.
4 Accounts and business.

KAL orientation

This project was planned with KAL as its basis, that is as an array of texts, all used in the same context, but with different purposes in that context. The children were asked to devise their texts with purposes in view. The basic question was 'What does a menu, or a shopping list have to be like to be useful and effective?'

Texts to be treated

The following list covers the texts envisaged at the outset:

notices;
shopping list;
recipe;
menu;
waiter's order pad;
customer's bill;
accounts;
business letter to bank manager asking for loan;
advertisements;
waiter asking for and taking customer's order;
customer paying cashier;
waiter's order to sandwich makers;

cashier and committee calculating and entering takings;
publicity song;
group rehearsals of waiter's talk;
committee meetings.

Some detailed advice was given for the writing of the business letter, but otherwise the teachers aimed to confine their comments to questions and discussions of fitness of devised texts for purpose.

14.1 Relationships among café texts

In a group, look at the relationships among the café texts, and draw a diagram to show these. Besides any ideas you have as a group bear in mind:

a   texts which have a sequential relationship;
b   texts which are drafts for other texts;
c   texts which have the same or overlapping content but different purposes;
d   texts which occur simultaneously;
e   texts which are developed by several people without prior planning. (Is there *no* prior planning at all?)

Assessment 1

The project presented children with tasks, and the actual goal of running a mini-enterprise, so that within three weeks (three Fridays) they had to cover their costs and make enough profit to repay the fifty pounds lent to them, not in the event by a bank, but by the Parent Teachers' Association. The following ATs were addressed:

AT 1	L3(b)	Convey an accurate message.
	L3(c)	Listening, responding and questioning in groups (i.e. in dealing with orders).
	L3(c)	Listening, responding, questioning in groups (i.e. in committee discussions).
	L3(d)	Giving, receiving and following precise instructions (i.e. waiter to kitchen).
	L4(b)	Development of L3(c).
	L4(c)	Development of L3(c).
	L4(d)	Participating in a presentation (e.g. menu, notice, waiter's pad).
	L5(b)	Development of L4(b).
	L5(c)	Development of L3(b) and L3(d).
	L5(d)	Development of L4(d).
	L5(e)	Recognising functional variation (vocabulary). (This partially involved standard English and tone necessary for a waiter.)

14.2 Statements of attainment: AT 3

Go through all the strands cited from AT 3, looking at the ENC formulation, and give examples of specific activities in the café project which would fulfil them, and show how KAL is entailed.

AT 2	L3(f)	Selecting and using appropriate information (i.e. in selecting and pricing ingredients).
	L4(d)	Development of L3(f).
	L5(c)	Distinguishing fact from opinion (i.e. in making price list different from menu and ads).
	L5(d)	Development of L4(d).
	L5(e)	Showing awareness of effect of choice of words (i.e. in drafting and editing ads, menus, business letter).

14.3 Statements of attainment: ATs 2 and 3

Go through all the strands cited from AT 2 and relate them to specific activities in the café project, and show how KAL is entailed.

AT 3	L3(a)	Producing texts with complete sentences, and some capital letters.
	L3(d)	Simple non-chronological writing.
	L3(c)	Drafting and checking.
	L4(a)	Development of L3(a).
	L4(c)	Development of L3(d).
	L4(d)	Begin using standard English structures.
	L4(e)	Discussing and redrafting.
	L5(a)	Using a range of genres oriented to reader.
	L5(c)	Development of L4(d).
	L5(d)	Drafting and editing on VDU.
	L5(e)	Varying vocabulary according to genre.
AT 4	L3(a)	Polysyllables used in work.
	L3(d)	Checking texts for spelling.
	L4(a)	Master main patterns of English.
AT 4/5	L5(a)	Spelling 'words of greater complexity' (e.g. 'café', 'sandwich').
	L5(b)	Development of L3(d).
	L5(c)	Producing clear writing.

14.4 Statements of attainment: ATs 4 and 5

Show how each of the strands cited can be realised in specific activities which promote KAL.

14.5 Statements of attainment: AT 1

Take two examples from each of Boxes 14.2–14.4 and show how they form content-texts, and which strands in AT 1 would underlie the related KAL-text.

Chronological writing

A number of ATs in the reading profile were not met, primarily because these expressly stipulate fiction and chronological writing. All the texts in the project were non-chronological.

This could have been rectified with a further piece of work after the project had been done, in which the children wrote up a report and assessment of the project. This was considered, and it was planned to make a video of the café in action and then get the children to write a narrative script/commentary to go with it.

A video-tape of the café in action was made, and shown, and a set of photos taken. However, the narrative report was not undertaken because there was not enough time at the end of term. This was a shortcoming, since it certainly would have been valuable to have a review of the project as a whole.

14.6 Chronological writing

1 Supplementing the café project

Outline a programme of work to supplement what has been described in this chapter for non-chronological texts. The supplementation should introduce chronological texts and make use of either photography or video filming.

2 ATs

Allocate ATs and strands not already cited, and relate these to specific activities which would promote KAL.

---

15 | *Codes*

Idea conceived in terms of KAL

This programme differs from the story making and café project in that it focuses on KAL as factual knowledge. The underlying idea was to get children to think in very general terms about the way in which language works, what a language is, and to approach these questions by thinking about codes.

15.1 Codes and language

1   Halliday describes language as a three-level type of code, in which what the person wants to communicate (discourse) is encoded as grammar and vocabulary (form), which is then encoded into physical speech sounds or written symbols (substance).[1]

2   Halliday uses the analogy of the traffic lights to illustrate this. Make your own interpretation of this analogy and show how a set of traffic lights has levels of:
   a   meaning;
   b   wording (i.e. vocabulary and combinations of vocabulary);
   c   physical expression;
   d   how the interpretation of this 'language' depends on context.

3   Devise a similar system of instructions to use with the children, and which the children can develop themselves. This system should be based on musical notes and/or instruments, for example:

Low note: 'sit down'
High note: 'stand up'

Use other musical signs for 'lie down', 'sit up', 'walk', 'run'.

   The work was conceived as a whole infant and junior project in which a range of texts were used.[2] The following are examples:

picture story;
musical score;
mime;
rebus writing;
ciphers;
animal communication;

backslang;
syntax.

The aim was for children to be given problem-solving tasks connected to code-making, code-using and code-breaking, and for this work to be related, as appropriate to age and development, to the way in which a language itself is structured like a code.

The code-like nature of language is exhibited in the relationship among linguistic levels. The sound encodes grammatical structure and vocabulary. Grammatical structure and vocabulary encode meanings.

Making a musical score (Key Stage 1)

Year 1 children composed a piece of music using cymbals, tambourines, a xylophone and an electronic keyboard. The music went with a dance/mime/drama representing aspects of the life of Henry Williamson's salmon in the story *Salar the Salmon*. The music had to represent the flowing water of the river, rocks, waving weeds, the menacing pike, the insidious lamphrey, the darting of young salmon, the leaping of adult salmon over the weir, and so on.

15.2 Score as code

1   How is a score like a code? Consider:
    a   how many strata or levels there are;
    b   what sort of discourse, or 'meaning', it has;
    c   what sorts of linguistic utterance it most resembles.

2   What would the 'grammar' of the musical score be like? Imagine you are making a score for some children to make music to represent the flowing of a river, the waterfall, rocks, kinds of fish, widening and slowing, and so on. Write a very simple score with a 'grammar' which deals with:
    a   the kind of sound (rhythm, volume, etc.) to be made with percussion instruments;
    b   which instruments are to play together and when;
    c   the sequence of musical 'turns';
    d   when players start and stop.

3   The score should show the overall shape of the piece and have a key for the symbols used.

4   Make a MICS analysis of the score.

In order to coordinate who plays when and what sort of impressionistic sounds – glissando up and down the xylophone for sunlight on the water, for example – a score was needed. The children had to devise a set of symbols which indicated aspects of Salar's journey up the river. This was done in the form of a spiral. The conductor points first to the middle and then moves his stick round and outwards, keeping a watch on the mime/dancers, and directing the musicians to change from 'sunlight on the water' to 'pike menace' and so on. The score had to serve a practical purpose and so had to be designed appropriately. For example, it had to be sufficiently large for the musicians to be able to see it at a distance, and the symbols needed to be clearly distinguishable from each other.

Sioux picture narrative

An example of a picture narrative done by Key Stage 2 children in Year 5 and Year 6 is given in Figure 15.1. Like the score, the Sioux picture narrative moves in a spiral beginning at the centre (see Figure 15.2). The picture the children did, although based on the Sioux one, uses a left to right top to bottom convention.

Figure 15.1 *Children's picture narrative*

Yes, some good ideas here

I think the alien must have come out of the flying saucer. Is that right?

And then the sunny day changes to rain because of the crash?

The man must be shouting to the girl about what has happened. Or is he warning her about something?

Row on a boat!?

Two children walked to the libary they saw a boy run home throw the woods. He saw a flying saucer crash Blimph in to the woods. It was a hot day. An alien rode on his buggy a man shouted at the girl over the hill. It was a dull day and it was raining. The alien ran into the woods on a boat.

FINISH

Figure 15.2 *Sioux picture narrative*

The devising was difficult at first because many of the children began by writing out a story and then translating it into symbols word by word. But this difficulty was productive because it brought out an essential difference between picturing and writing or speaking a language; namely that with picture narration there is no one-to-one correspondence between word and symbol. A question which the children were asked to discuss was what language a Sioux picture story was in. The point here, of course, is that pictures can be explained or 'read' in any language so long as you know the picture syntax and vocabulary.

Syntax

This work was done after the Year 5/6 children had done the picture narrative, and other kinds of code such as a music code, rebus writing, and 'secret' ciphers based on replacing particular letters in messages, using the computer.

The syntax was done by taking a short sentence from messages already used and the teacher cutting it up into grammatical components.[3] For example, the sentence (clause) could be: 'The Sioux leader was riding his horse through the dark forest secretly.' The components provided were:

the Sioux leader
was
riding

his horse
through the dark forest
at night
secretly

Each of these had a distinctive colour to indicate what kind of grammatical structure it was. Figure 15.3 sets this out:

Figure 15.3 *Colour and shape coding of strips*

STRIP	STRUCTURE	COLOUR
The Sioux leader	nominal group	blue
was	auxiliary verb	red
riding	lexical verb	green
his red horse	nominal group	blue
through the dark forest	prepositional phrase	yellow
at night	prepositional phrase	yellow
secretly	adverbial group	brown

Other components provided for further work were items to be used for substitution:

it	(blue)
he	(blue)
there	(brown)
then	(brown)
did	(green)

The first task the children were given was simply to make up as many different clauses by rearranging the components.

The appeal of this work – which children of all ages find absorbing – is primarily aesthetic, of course, that is, being ingenious with patterns, and stretching language to the limits.

15.3 Grammar as interpretation

1 Word groups

Photocopy the following word groups. Paste them onto strips of strong card coloured as indicated:

The Sioux leader	(blue)
was	(red)
riding	(green)
his horse	(blue)
through the dark forest	(yellow)
at night	(yellow)

secretly	(brown)
then	(brown)

2　The children make up utterances which fulfil the following contextual purposes. They may make adjustments to individual words by removing or adding 'ing' etc.:

a　the title of the story;

b　an instruction;

c　an utterance which relies entirely on the reader already knowing what is being talked about;

d　a question;

e　an answer to the question 'Who was travelling through the dark forest all night?';

f　paraphrasing 'The Sioux leader was travelling through a dark forest all night' without mentioning who was travelling or referring to the person as 'he'.

3　Assessment

How would you justify this sort of work from the point of view of:

a　general education?

b　KAL?

c　ENC?

Assessment of idea

Approaching KAL directly as fact is controversial in the sense that Cox recommends that KAL be conceived as an aspect of some other work. But the examples of KAL given in the Non-statutory Guidance Section of ENC are, in fact, conceived in terms of linguistics. The codes project is, in effect, 'linguistics for kids'. Hence it must be considered as a cross-curricular project, since linguistics as a body of thinking draws upon aspects of science, maths, sociology, anthropology and psychology, as well as English.

One aim of thinking about codes is to develop categorising and observing skills typical of the sciences. Although the orientation here is towards content, the way in which the work was carried out was to present children with practical and conceptual problems to solve, and to get them to formulate the generalisations which suited them. So the actual sessions were not oriented towards the memorising and application of abstruse terminology. And the problem-solving format gave ample scope for oral discussion, text devising and interpretation.

A problem in assessing this work was that it was difficult to find strands in ENC which directly focused on the fundamentals of language: that a language is both like and unlike animal communications or man-made codes. Hence a teacher who feels that all work must be justified specifically from entries in ENC may hesitate to do this work, which is a pity because from the point of view of general good practice and general language awareness it was felt to be very promising.

Notes

1   In the event it was done as two separate programmes – one (Sioux picture stories) with a class of top junior children in Years 5 and 6, devoted to codes and KAL as such, the other (musical score) done with two Year 2 infants classes as part of a project based on an adaptation of Henry Williamson's novel, *Salar the Salmon*.

2   'Modes of Meaning and Modes of Expression: types of grammatical structure and their determination by different semantic functions' in *Function and Context in Linguistic Analysis: essays offered to William Haas* (1979), edited by D. J. Allerton, Edward Carney and David Holdcroft (Cambridge: Cambridge University Press, pp. 57–79).

3   Compare Box 11.7.

PART SIX
Wider perspectives

Part Six outlines some of the implications of KAL: the implications of the textual approach to whole-school curriculum design, the centrality of KAL to contemporary learning, and the peculiar status of poetry in relation to KAL. No more is attempted here than to raise these questions in a general form.

16 | *Knowledge about language across the curriculum*

The textual approach to language and 'subjects'

What has been said about KAL has been confined to work which would traditionally be considered a part of the 'English' curriculum, or the language component of theme work. Implicit in a theme-based approach to primary work is the idea that all kinds of learning can be treated from the point of view of language; an implicit recognition that whatever is done in school is textual. Every classroom activity is an array of texts, spoken and/or written.

The textuality of learning may be obscured by the way in which traditional school 'subjects' such as maths or history, are characterised: that is, in terms of their content. But English is not a 'subject' in this sense. It has no particular content.[1] This holds even if we think of English as the study of literature. Poems and novels are not defined by their content either. But a maths lesson, or a maths calculation can be described in terms of the texts used just as a language or English lesson can.

Yet, once this has been realised, it will also be realised that the difference traditionally assumed between 'subjects' and English rests on a relative neglect of the way in which maths or history is, in fact, carried by texts; that content can never in fact be studied 'in itself'. Although a maths session can be thought of in terms of content, the process of teaching and learning are matters of medium, interaction and setting. When we learn maths we are learning 'the language of maths'.

16.1 Technology as knowledge about language
Make a MICS analysis of the following imagined texts in which two children are working with a simple electrical circuit:
a Discussing how to connect the wires to battery and bulb to make the light come on.
b Drafting a report as to what they discovered.

16.2 Text and lesson prep
1 How far could a lesson preparation be done simply as a set of MICS analyses of the texts to be used, together with an indication of sequence and simultaneity?

2 Sketch a plan for the work outlined in Box 16.1 including such texts as:
a teacher's introductory explanation as to what to do;

b practical work on getting into groups together with discussion as to who goes where, and remainders;
c collaborative planning and drawing of a diagram with stick figures (or photos) to show the different permutations possible in a group of five.

3 Assessment
Assign ENC strands, one from each of ATs 1, 2, and 3.

A maths text

The following sketch of a MICS analysis (Figure 16.1) represents part of a session introducing Year 1 infants to the notion of 'remainder' in arithmetic. They arrange themselves into groups of this or that number specified by the teacher, and see how many groups there are, and whether there are children left over as 'remainder'.

Figure 16.1 *Maths text on remainders*

G E N R E	MEDIUM	INTERACTION	CONTENT	SETTING
	speech movement gestures	exploratory group discussion, inference	maths division remainders	cleared space in classroom or in gym

Cross-curricular planning

The planning of all schoolwork could be done in a textual way, every session being planned as an array of texts. What the children learn, then, is a repertoire of genres. These will differ because the traditional subjects are associated with particular combinations of MICS (that is, with genres), and in particular with different kinds of medium organisation: the way a maths calculation coheres and is set out, differs from that of a poem, or a historical document.

There is an adage in teaching that 'every teacher is a language teacher'. A corollary to this is that all learning is language learning. In other words the actual assimilation of the concept of remainders by children is achieved by their talking through the idea among themselves and learning to operate the discourse and vocabulary required to talk about remainders, and make it part of their own repertoire. Knowing about remainders, in effect, amounts to being able to engage in texts about remainders, and not just one kind of text such as the division sum, but a range of texts which vary in medium interaction and setting. The same general point can be made about all 'subjects' on the curriculum.

Problems

There are two kinds of problem which these comments raise. The first is that, when it comes to curriculum planning, it appears at first sight to place the language coordinator in a school in a very special position. Everything depends on texts, and they are the expert in language. At the level of personalities this could well pose problems in the short-term. But the special position accorded to language in the curriculum is, in part, just a result of the approach through textuality itself. Once it is recognised that all learning occurs in and through textual interaction, it will also be realised that the maths coordinator or the science coordinator is in a privileged position when it comes to talking about the textual repertoire of their areas of study. The theoretical development of the textual approach has, in fact, always been multi-disciplinary.[2]

The second problem is an ideological one. The textual approach is associated not necessarily with socialist or left approaches to education, but it does conflict with the approach to learning which lays special emphasis on 'facts', and regards fact as, in principal, separable from and 'prior to' argument, exploration and discussion. To prioritise 'facts' in this way does, of course, run counter to a textual or discourse approach to learning.

This problem is not just ideological, but political, like ENC itself. The textual approach runs counter to aspects of ENC, particularly its division into curricular 'subjects'. Taking up the wider implications of the textual approach, therefore, although it accords with much contemporary scholarship, it is all too likely to suffer the media over-simplification and deliberate manufacturing of controversy which has characterised other debates in education in recent years.

Notes

1 Of course, this is a false contrast, but more generally accepted of subjects such as science or history than in art or music which can be thought of more as 'languages'.
2 See, for example, the works of Michel Foucault whose textual approach has been applied to knowledge as such, to imprisonment, medicine and sex. See his *The Archeology of Knowledge* (1969) translated by A. N. Sheridan Smith (London: Tavistock Publications).

17 | *Poetry*

Poetic language

KAL can be taught in a transmissional way, as a body of facts, in effect as primary school linguistics. In this mode it is best thought of as science or social science. The approach taken in this book has, however, focused primarily on the process by which texts are devised and how they are related to contextual purposes. And much of this work has been justified along aesthetic lines, though this has been connected with the justifications for KAL given in the Kingman and Cox reports that KAL can enhance textual practice.

Poetic language[1] is of particular interest here because it requires the reader/hearer to register not just *what* the poet is talking about but also, simultaneously, and as part of the overall impact of the text, *how* it is expressed, the processes by which the text has been produced, as a craft. When Keats writes:

> 'Forlorn. The very word is like a bell
> to toll me back from thee to my sole self.'

he makes us respond not just to the meaning of the word 'forlorn', but to its sound and associations, the repeated long vowel is taken up in the repeated long vowels of 'toll' and 'sole'. The pattern is more complex than this, but essentially produces a bell-like tolling from the alternation of the sounds of 'el' and 'ole' in 'bell, toll' and 'sole, self'. In other words the passage is not just about the nightingale's song, it is also *about language*. Such texts provide what might be termed 'KAL in process'. Here, responding to language as meaning and knowing about language as sound, come together.

The idea that poetry and KAL should go together is not set out as a concession to children. It forms part of the contemporary intellectual debate about language. The semiotician, Julia Kristeva proposes, for example, that poetic language should be established as 'the object of linguistics' attention in its pursuit of truth in language'.[2] Poetry provides a way of exploring language, and through that, the way a culture hangs together.

Poetry and literacy

Poetry provides scope for the development of early literacy since poems can be very short and so allow close attention to a small number of words which are interesting, perhaps funny, and form an actual communication with scope also for performance. Poems or related short texts such as advertisements, jokes and riddles, are thus more versatile than most story books.

Such a text is both a 'whole text' which gives scope to the reader to construct meaning imaginatively, and it is also a text in which attention is drawn to details of sounds, and phonics. Poetic texts thus allow the teacher to bring together phonic awareness and reading for meaning. Attention to both is generically required. And this sort of awareness applies right through a person's reading, and applies at all levels.

At the levels of early literacy, poetry is valuable again because it is often rhythmically memorable and repetitive. This makes it suitable for the development of reading strategies at all three textual levels, to sound, to wording, and to meaning. Repeated texts are easy to produce from almost any piece of language a child may present. For example, the comment 'I rode to school on my bike this morning' can be turned into a series of lines for a rap. The child can simply repeat them to the beat, or grammatical structure can be kept steady while just a few individual words are changed. Thus;

'I rode to school on my bike this morning
I rode to school on my bike today.
I rode the road on my wheels today.
I rode the sunrays on whizzing wheels.'

The attractiveness of this kind of 'reader' is that it gives learners some control over their learning, and at the same time enhances their consciousness, explicitly, of how language works, since they have to devise the parallelism.

Aesthetic and cultural dimensions

Teaching language through poetry and poetry as knowledge about language in process, allows quite young children an insight into literature which can be developed in the same vein throughout their education. Indeed, the way in which poetic texts are read overlaps with the model of reading which we have employed, and which emphasises reading *into* texts and imaginative constructions of their meanings.[3] Not only that, their learning to read will encompass reading *into* texts of all kinds.

Poetry also brings together the aesthetic and cultural dimensions which Kingman and Cox have cited as justifications for KAL. Reading poetry not only draws attention to textual processes; it relates details of language to very wide cultural issues. The ability to engage in a poetic text has a further application in the social and political sphere, since the skills developed allow people to see how, for different ends, politicians and journalists play fast and loose with language, not to make us see more deeply into our culture or minds, but in order to deceive. The language of the poet and the language of the media politician are closely related because they are opposites. The politician hopes, all too often, that the listeners will not look too closely into his textual organisation; the poet hopes they will.

An aesthetic understanding of KAL gives children at least a chance of reading media texts 'aesthetically', that is to look into the ways in which they have been produced, and their purposes.

Notes

1 The term 'poetic language' is wider than the term 'poetry'. Poetic language occurs in a range of texts, where in some way linguistic patterning draws attention to the process by which the text has been produced, to 'language itself'. The classical expression of this idea, now very widely accepted, is 'Concluding Statement: Linguistics and Poetics' by Roman Jakobson (1960), in *Style in Language* edited by T. A. Sebeok (New York: John Wiley).

2 *Desire in Language* (1980) by Julia Kristeva, edited by Leon S. Roudiez, translated by Thomas Gora, Alice Jardine, and Leon S. Roudiez (Oxford: Basil Blackwell) p. 25.

3 See, for example, *The Meaning Makers: Children Learning Language and Using Language to Learn* (1986) by Gordon Wells (London: Hodder and Stoughton).

Bibliography

ALTHUSSER, L. (1971) 'Ideology and Ideological State Apparatuses' in *Lenin and Philosophy*. London: New Left Books.

BARRS, M. (1990) *Words Not Numbers: Assessment in English*. Exeter: NATE Short Run Press.

BARNES, D. (1976) *From Communication to Curriculum*. Harmondsworth, Middlesex: Penguin.

BARTHES, R. (1977) *Image-Music-Text*. London: Fontana.

BARTHES, R. (1983) *Mythologies*. St. Albans: Paladin.

BERGER, P. and LUCKMANN, I. (1967) *The Social Construction of Reality*. Harmondsworth: Penguin Books.

BERRY, M. (1975, 1977) *Introduction to Systemic Linguistics* (two volumes). London: Batsford.

BRADLEY, L. (1990) 'Rhyming Connections in Learning to Read and Spell' in *Children's Difficulties in Reading, Spelling and Writing* edited by Peter D. Pumphrey and Colin D. Elliott. London: Falmer Press (pp. 83–100).

CARTER, R. and BURTON, D. (1982) *Literary Text and Language*. London: Edward Arnold.

CATALDO, S. and ELLIS, N. (1990) 'Learning to Spell, Learning to Read' in *Children's Difficulties in Reading, Spelling and Writing* edited by Peter D. Pumphrey and Colin D. Elliott. London: Falmer Press (pp. 101–25).

CAZDEN, C.; CORDEIRO, P. and GIACOMBEE, M. E. (1985) 'Spontaneous and Scientific Concepts: Young Children's Learning of Punctuation' in *Language and Learning: An Interactional Perspective* edited by Gordon Wells and John Nichols. London: Falmer Press.

CHANDLER, R. (1988) 'Unproductive Busywork' in *English in Education*, 22, 3, 20–8.

CHRISTIE, F. (1983) 'Learning to Write: a process of learning how to mean' in *English in Australia*, 66, 4–17.

CHRISTIE, F. (1986) 'Writing in Schools: Generic structures as ways of meaning' in *Functional Approaches to Writing* edited by B. Couture. London: Frances Pinter.

CHRISTIE, F. (1989) *Language Education*. London: Oxford University Press.

COULTHARD, M. and MONTGOMERY, M. (1981) (eds) *Studies in Discourse Analysis*. London: Routledge and Kegan Paul.

COWARD, R. and ELLIS, J. (1971) *Language and Materialism*. London: Routledge and Kegan Paul.

CULLER, J. (1975) *Structuralist Poets*. London: Routledge and Kegan Paul.

DES (1975) *A Language for Life*: Report of the Committee of Inquiry appointed by the Secretary of State for Education and Science (Bullock Report) London: HMSO.

FOUCAULT, M. (1969) *The Archaeology of Knowledge*, translated by A. M. Sheridan Smith. London: Tavistock Publications.

GREGORY, M. and CARROL, S. (1978) *Language and Situation: Language Varieties in their Social Contexts*. London: Routledge and Kegan Paul.

HALLIDAY, M. A. K. (1978) *Language as Social Semiotic*. London: Edward Arnold.

HALLIDAY, M. A. K. (1979) 'Modes of Meaning and Modes of Expression: types of grammatical structure and their determination by different semantic functions' in *Function and Context in Linguistic Analysis: essays offered to William Haas* edited by D. J. Allerton, Edward Carney and David Holdcroft. Cambridge: Cambridge University Press (pp. 57–79).

HALLIDAY, M. A. K. (1985) *Spoken and Written Language*. London: Oxford University Press.

HALLIDAY, M. A. K. and HASAN, R. (1989) *Language, Context and Text: Aspects of Language in a Social Semiotic Perspective*. London: Oxford University Press.

HARPIN, W. (1979) 'Attitudes to Language and Language Teaching' in *English in Education* 12, 2.

HAYNES, J. (1989) *Introducing Stylistics*. London: Unwin Hyman.

HEATON, J. B. (1971) *Practice through Picture: drills in English sentence patterns*. London: Longman.

KRESS, G. and HODGE, R. (1969) *Language as Ideology*. London: Routledge and Kegan Paul.

KRESS, G. (1979) 'The Social Values of Speech and Writing' by Gunther Kress in *Language and Control* by Roger Fowler, Bob Hodge, Gunther Kress, Tony Trew. London: Routledge and Kegan Paul (pp. 46–62).

KRISTEVA, J. (1980) *Desire in Language* edited by Leon S. Roudiez, translated by Thomas Gora, Alice Jardine, and Leon S. Roudiez. Oxford: Basil Blackwell (p. 25).

LABOV, L. (1967) 'Narrative Analysis: oral versions of personal experience' in *Essays on the Verbal and Visual Arts* edited by June Helm. Seattle: University of Washington Press.

LEMKE, J. L. (1989) *Using Language in the Classroom*. London: Oxford University Press.

MACAULEY, W. J. (1947) 'The Difficulty of Grammar' in *Journal of Educational Psychology*, 17.

MACKAY, D., THOMPSON, B. and SCHAUB, P. (1970) *Breakthrough to Literacy*. Harlow: Longman/ Schools Council.

MARTIN, J. R. (1989) *Factual Writing: Exploring and Challenging Social Reality*. London: Oxford Unviersity Press.

McCABE, C. (1988) *Futures for English*. Manchester: Manchester University Press.

MEEK, M. (1982) *Learning to Read*. London: The Bodley Head.

MEEK, M. (1988) *How Texts Teach What Readers Learn*. London: Thimble Press.

MEEK, M. and MILLS, C. (1988) (eds) *Language and Literacy in the Primary School*. London: Falmer Press.

NEWMAN, J. (1985) *Whole Language: Theory in Use*. London: Heinemann.

ONG, W. (1982) *Orality and Literacy: The Technologizing of the World*. London: Methuen.

PRATT, M. L. (1977) *Towards and Speech Act Theory of Literacy Discourse*. Bloomington: Indiana University Press.

PUMPHREY, P. D. and ELLIOTT, C. D. (1990) *Children's Difficulties in Reading, Spelling and Writing*. London: Falmer Press.

READ, C. (1986) *Children's Creative Spelling*. London: Routledge and Kegan Paul.

ROSEN, H. (1990) 'The Nationalisation of English' address to NATE '90 Conference, University of Manchester, 11 April.

ROSEN, M. (1989) *Did I Hear You Write?* London: Andre Deutsch.

SEARLE, J. (1969) *Speech Acts*. Cambridge: Cambridge University Press.

SMITH, F. (1978) *Reading*. Cambridge: Cambridge University Press.

STUBBS, M. (1983) *Discourse Analysis: The Sociolinguistic Analysis of Natural Language*. Oxford: Basil Blackwell.

TRUDGILL, P. (1975) *Accent, Dialect and the School*. London: Edward Arnold.

TRUDGILL, P. (1975) *On Dialect*. Oxford: Basil Blackwell.

WATERLAND, L. (1988) *Read with Me*. London: Thimble Press.

WELLS, G. (1985) *Language and Learning: An Interactional Perspective* (edited by Gordon Wells and John Nichols). London: Falmer Press.

WELLS, G. (1986) *The Meaning Makers: Children Learning Language and Using Language to Learn*. London: Hodder and Stoughton.

Index